Novice Negotiator

How to Job Hunt in Tech Without Leaving Money on the Table

Table of Contents

Introduction

I've spent the last fifteen years of my life working in the tech industry, and a lot of my time there has been spent in interviews— either going on them or conducting them. *Novice Negotiator* is the result of my experiences. It grew from a collection of tips that I continued to give over the years to my friends, colleagues, and direct reports. After a while it became apparent that there are widespread issues when it comes to effectively and accurately recruiting in tech, and I wanted to help shed some light for people who are new to the world of getting a job in tech, arming them with advice and strategies for acing interviews and negotiating fair salaries.

I have done my best to outline the landscape and strategies to use to your advantage in this book, and rather than provide a caveat for each piece of advice, I'll do it up front here for everything. I am not a scientist. While I did research, I did not do any experiments. Several of the examples in this book are anecdotes. Several of the situations work out the way they do because of chance, biases, or other qualities specific to the scenarios. That said, there is enough knowledge in this book that I hope most, if not all, of it is useful.

At its core, *Novice Negotiator* was written to arm the reader with a series of communication tools, professionalism tips, and job-hunting strategies to enable getting higher-paying jobs in tech. The current tech recruiting scene is unstructured enough that someone with advanced knowledge of the situation can protect themselves from amateur pitfalls and obtain higher salaries at whatever tiered job they have.

This guide provides a solid explanation of the unstructured hiring situation, along with several mini-guides to the path to getting and keeping a job (résumés, phone screens, interviews, recruiter negotiation, and networking after you have a job). Additionally, I hope to shed some light on a few myths that keep people from making beneficial decisions in their current careers.

It is my sincerest hope that this book provides valuable insider information to the people that read it.

Happy hunting!

Ryan Lockard, 2017

Chapter One:
Welcome to the Real World

"The most common way people give up their power is by thinking they don't have any." — Alice Walker

In this chapter, I'll be looking at how things really are once you're part of the workforce. What did they skip in college? Was there discussion of salary ranges? Did anyone mention that your peers' salaries are hidden and this is used against you? How long should you ideally stay at a job? Did anyone tell you "trying hard" doesn't get you anywhere at all if your boss doesn't think you're someone they can grab a beer with? Do you have any idea what your day-to-day is going to be like in the real world?

The fact is, after college there's no longer a defined support system—each individual company cares about you only during the time that you work there. That being the case, how can you compete against the existing recruiting and hiring engine that's already set up?

The scope of *Novice Negotiator* is to assist those who are completely new to the tech scene, perhaps people who prefer not to think about the job hunt, as well as to assist those who may have been around for a while but don't have a strong grasp of how much they should be getting paid—or how to negotiate for it. I'll take you through all the steps, from cleaning up your résumé, how and where to hunt online, what to do during phone screens, and how to handle interviews, as well as how to actually negotiate. This book's single-minded strategy is to help you understand the entire hiring process from the recruiter side, so you'll know what leverage you need to have from the get-go.

But first, let's set the stage with a short story that likely will seem very familiar.

Your First Job!

You did it! You made it through that grueling four to five years of studying, drinking, and skipping just enough classes not to fail. Now it's time to get a job. Did you have some internships? A co-op? Great! No? Start over, go back to college and good luck. In the tech world, internships and co-ops are crucially important experiences to have, so if you didn't have either, hopefully your mom's friends are looking for junior-level folks and you'll get lucky enough that one will hire you despite your lack of experience.

Ready now? Great! Let's walk you through your first job. During your final semester in college, you'll begin talking with your current internship sponsor. If you're lucky, they'll stop paying you $12 an hour and offer you a salary. You won't even think of negotiating, assuming they're paying whatever their book or HR department said the salary was. The internal recruiter will simply say, "We can bring you on at $38,000 a year, here, sign this," and it'll sound like it's a fact, like it's something that the recruiter is just passing along. You sign the paper because how you could even be arrogant enough to negotiate? Besides, they might just retract the deal if you say something. Better just sign and know you have a job! And surely if you work hard at this company you'll get rewarded with bonuses and promotions. That's how it works, right?

Time to start that daily grind. How's that team you're working with? Tolerable? Kinda funny? Good, good. How's your manager? You like him? It's definitely a guy, by the way. Oh, you have a new one? That was quick. How are the daily standups? Did you go to any happy hours yet? It's only been five months and they're doing a re-org? That's tough. Either way, I'm sure your constant output and dedication will be noticed by the important people upstairs.

How was the holiday party? You got a little tipsy? That's okay, as long as you didn't say anything embarrassing I'm sure you'll still get that stellar raise.

Your department launched a big project? That's great! Congratulations. Did they notice all the cool stuff you did? You're not sure? Well, as long as you were a team player. Bonuses definitely are tied to how well and how hard you work. Definitely.

Bonus time! That's great—but oh, you have a new manager again? Hmm, I hope your last manager left enough notes taken during your one-on-ones. Oh, you didn't really have one-on-ones? And you didn't have clear goals? Or maybe you had clear goals but they didn't really matter? I'm sorry, but be happy with the 2% raise they gave you. Now you're almost over $40,000. I'm sure next year you'll get a promotion. Keep plugging away, kid. We'll get there.

Oh no, they had a bad year? They can't pay out bonuses? I'm sorry. Well, it'll pick up next year.

Another so-so year? That's it, let's go get a new job.

Your friend says their place is really great to work at. Awesome. What's the pay? They're offering you $41,000? Well, it's better than where you are.

Your Second Job!
You did it! You made it through that grueling two to three years of showing up to work, meaningless emails, and even more meaningless meetings!

Let me walk you through your second job. Your friend who got you in the door is great, but you don't really ever see them. They're on another team. Or maybe you see them all the time, and you realize they're not that much of a friend. Either way, a job's a job. You got out of that terrible mess that wasn't paying you what you were worth, and now it's your time to shine! Good thing you negotiated your salary this time around. Oh, wait, you forgot to do that part. You were desperate, and scared they wouldn't hire you, so you just accepted whatever they opened with.

Oh well, let's start the daily grind again. How's that team you're working with? Tolerable again? A little funnier? Good, good. How's your manager? You have one-on-ones with them this time? That's great! Oh, they cancel and reschedule them a lot? That's okay, I'm sure they really care about you.

How was the holiday party? You got a little tipsy again? That's okay, as long as you didn't say anything embarrassing I'm sure you'll get that stellar raise this time.

Your department launched a big project? That's great! Congratulations. Did they notice all the cool stuff you did? You're not sure? Well, as long as you were a team player.

Bonus time! That's great—wait, you have a new manager yet again? At least they gave you a raise though. Be happy with the 2% they gave you. Now you're almost over $43,000. I'm sure next year you'll get a promotion.

They had a bad year? I'm sorry. Well, it'll pick up some time.

Another mediocre year? That's it, let's go get a third job.

Your other buddy says their place is really great to work at? Awesome. What's the pay? They're offering $52,000? Well, it's better than where you are …

The Ugly Truth

The above story is somewhat exaggerated, but still within the realm of possibility. I'm sure it hit home with many of you. This situation is exactly what this book is trying to solve. The education pipeline focuses on a certain things deemed important, like history, math, sciences, art—educational subjects we all hope to turn into a relevant job. However, among the pieces that education does not account for are certain "real world skills"—including things like what your salary should be at any given job.

This situation becomes exacerbated when you get all the way through college and then even into the actual job—there's no career path training whatsoever. Your initial boss may or may not care about your career advancement. Or even worse, they might care deeply but not actually have the power or time to focus on it, leaving you with promise after promise that leads nowhere. You have to learn through experience, which can mean several years of trial and error, or perhaps several years before you have any idea that you're not making a solid amount of money for your work. Those are years you won't get back. There are no free retries in the career business.

There are a few contributors to this "casual" scenario. One is salaries and who sets them. The fact is that salaries are private. There's no book where you can find out exactly what a company's range is. It's a conflict of interest for them to let you know what your coworkers are being paid. For some reason there's a social stigma on "talking money," and this is used against individuals regularly. In the past few years, a few online services have sprung up that allow you to search salaries in a given area within a certain field. Those sites are absolutely helpful, but it's not like you can use them as evidence while bargaining with a recruiter. What matters are your alternative offers compared to what they are negotiating with you.

Besides hidden salaries, another contributing factor is the design of the hiring process itself. You're completely on your own, each company is slightly different, and the recruiters appear to be your friends throughout the entire thing. You'll be passively pressured to make a decision quickly and be expected to accept the initial (low) offer that the company has provided. It's so subtle and matter-of-fact that early on you wouldn't even think countering their offer was an option.

If you're not paying attention, the real world is going to run you over. People who don't have your best interest at heart will be setting standards that you'll have to deal with for the rest of your life. If you're not careful, you could start your career already behind by a wide margin, and, worse, never even realize it.

Entry-Level Salaries

"According to GlassDoor.com, which gathered information from over 15,000 software developers, the national average entry level software developer salary is $55,000. That comes to approximately $26.44 per hour if you work forty hours a week. Some companies start software developers out below that number, as low as $50,000, and some start software developers out significantly higher than that, even as high as $91,000 annually.

"You can expect your salary to increase as you gain experience and longevity with an organization. On average, software developers max out at $124,000 nationwide, but many companies pay experienced software developers much more than that. An annual salary of $124,000 breaks down to approximately $59.62 hourly if you average forty hours a week."

http://www.codingdojo.com/blog/entry-level-software-developer-salary/

The Hiring Process

The hiring dance usually goes something like this:

(1) There's a single job you find, either through a job search, a referral, or a recruiter who finds you. It sounds perfect or at least good enough.

(2) At some point an extremely friendly recruiter will call you and talk up the job while asking about yourself; this person will not have a strong technical background and will only be able to talk about the workplace environment, or the type of applicant the hiring manager has told them they want for

the position. The recruiter may also say a certain number of buzzwords, asking if you are familiar with any of them. This list of words was also provided by the hiring manager—things like "microservices," "continuous integration," "white box testing," or "agile methodologies."

(3) The hiring manager and one other person will phone screen you. They will ask at most three technical questions, but really they're just trying to get a loose grasp of your skill level. As long as you don't sound like an idiot, they'll bring you in for an interview. This phone screen will likely go one of two ways: very awkwardly, as the hiring manager appears unprepared and fumbles around, or super casually, where they only ask high-level questions and seem very pleased with whatever answers you give. You may even feel smarter than the people screening you. They might try to oversell the position to you, and even sound extremely happy just to be chatting with you on the phone.

(4) You go in for an interview on-site. You'll likely talk with the two people who phone screened you, plus two to three more individuals—typically coworkers, the hiring manager, and the hiring manager's boss. The depth of the technical questions will vary, but it will only last about three hours tops, where you'll usually spending thirty minutes with each person. There is an outside chance that you'll be ambushed with four to five people all at once. Either way, the individual questions aren't likely to vary that much. "Tell me about yourself." "Why are you looking for a new job?" "What's your biggest weakness?" "How do you handle [insert incredibly common problem in your specific slice of the tech industry]?" Occasionally they may ask you to

describe what you bring to the table, or why they, the impressive company, should hire you, the lowly applicant, but that power dynamic has been drastically changing as tech companies become more and more desperate for any kind of talent with a pulse and a brain.

(5) Afterwards the recruiter will ask you point blank what your current salary is (even if they have asked already), and then offer you about 2-5% more than whatever you told them. They'll do this with a smile, and fully expect you to immediately accept the offer.

My thoughts as I dealt with the above experiences over the course of my career went a little something like this:

- "Oh, this must been how a small-time company works. I bet it won't be so informal next time."

- "Oh, this time must have been a fluke, I bet this larger company just hasn't invested much in hiring or recruiting."

- "Oh, this mistake must be what it's like because the recruiter is new or maybe the hiring manager is new."

- "Oh, this odd part must be because the vibe of this company is supposed to be super casual."

- "Oh, it's like this at a big, established company too? That's weird, I bet it's just this one."

- "Oh, it's like this everywhere? Hmm …"

It's certainly a standard reaction to assume that the large corporate entities know what they're doing and that you, the new person, fresh in the workforce, must clearly have missed something. How could they be so disorganized? They're a large company. People would get fired if they did their job wrong … right?

It took several of the exact same exchanges with multiple companies and recruiters for me to break out of that mold and realize that sometimes they might NOT know what they're doing. I'll touch on this in later chapters, but for now, rest assured that there isn't some army of trained recruiting professionals that are ready to chew you up and spit you out.

Salary Shortchange? Were you undercut out of the gate for your current tech job? See below for the typical entry-level pay. Regions can vary as much as +/- 15% roughly.

Job Title	Entry-Level Salary* (average across US)
QA Analyst	$49,035 per year
Web Developer	$51,000 per year
QA Engineer	$59,596 per year
IT Business Analyst	$60,000 per year
Software Developer	$62,000 per year
IT Project Manager	$68,000 per year

* from Payscale.com search results

Becoming a Novice Negotiator

We've gone over an experience that is shockingly common during the first three years of having a tech job. We've briefly touched on why this industry operates this way. The rest of *Novice Negotiator* will delve into how to defend against this situation, and more importantly, how to use it to your advantage. I'll spend the last chapters of this book discussing how to make the most of your job and how to plan out your career trajectory while making yourself more attractive to other potential employers.

Now, full disclosure: while I have done some limited research in this arena, but most of the advice in this book does not come from scientific experimentation. There were no double-blind randomized controlled trials to figure out how to best negotiate with a real-world recruiter. The bulk of the information comes from anecdotal experience and what has worked for specific individuals. Even if the specifics of the examples don't completely apply to you, there are enough useful rubrics and strategies throughout *Novice Negotiator* to the point that almost anyone will have something to gain from reading this book.

I set out to level some of the playing field, and impart knowledge that would have been incredibly useful back when I was starting out in the tech job sector.

Chapter Two:
The Lay of the Land

"It's so much easier to suggest solutions when you don't know too much about the problem."

— Malcolm Forbes

In this chapter, I'll be examining the recruiting situation in the tech industry and how it's changed (and not changed) within the past twenty years. How did things get this way (and were they always this bad?), and how can we use this information to our advantage?

A History Lesson: Younger Workforce

The heavy contributors in the tech workforce are getting younger and younger. Why? This isn't happening across most other industries. You don't find manual laborers at manufacturing plants getting younger and younger or an influx of agricultural companies cropping up with young Silicon Valley-style owners. Sales and marketing is only getting younger to account for social media (for relevant industries). There certainly isn't a swath of young lawyers representing people in courtrooms. Tech, compared to other industries, has a young workforce.

Accessibility of Tech

Via the internet, younger generations have access to tech now that they couldn't have in the 1980s and even in the 1990's. People can teach themselves, and quite frankly, most developers use Google and Stack Exchange to solve their problems in the workplace. What's to stop teenagers from learning from those same tools? For the first time in recent history, entry-level individuals have a heavy impact on the workforce contributions at companies. You don't have to wait five years and have three certifications before they let you commit code for production use (of course, there are some places still like this).

Social Views of Tech

Tech as we know it used to be wildly unpopular. If you were in tech, you were an engineer. It wasn't seen as a "regular" job—you were on par with a scientist who worked in a lab somewhere. The increase in accessibility helped create something of a feedback loop. As tech became more accessible, it became more popular, and more lucrative. Eventually the brogrammer stereotype showed up, which made it even more mainstream. All of this decreased the overall age of the workforce.

Bleeding Edge, Cheap Tech
Tech moves fast. Everyone is somewhat aware of this fact, but you have to think about why something like the speed of the industry's tools and internal products would impact hiring capabilities.

You can't vet experts of bleeding-edge tech. Part of this is because the bleeding-edge tech has only been out for two years. Since it is only two years old, of course anyone with the time can become "an expert." When the college-aged kid and the veteran software engineer apply for the same job, you can bet the recruiters are going to hire the new kid for pennies on the dollar when decades of experience aren't needed or even possible. Old tech has overhead and licensing fees too. Some new tech does as well, but there's also the advent of open-source or cheap closed-source startups that are dying to make a name for themselves. Ultimately, what this means is that you can no longer have an older person with twenty-plus years of experience in Pascal—it's just not possible for there to be that many years of experience with bleeding-edge tech—so the recruiters no longer have to find "super experts." Instead they can settle for someone who has dabbled in the tech that they're looking for.

The Systemic Problems: Salary and Career Advancement
No one else will ever care about your career advancement. In fact, there's a conflict of interest between your managers when it comes

to your salary and bonuses. They typically have to balance it throughout a department, a fact they rarely bring up.

The inadequacies of career pathing, goal setting, and properly valued rewards within a company are all so vast that these could be their own book. Again, a combination of factors are at play here. Some managers don't actually want to be managers. Some are just the most senior person around in terms of technical skill. Other managers have the greatest of intentions but there just isn't a support structure in place at the company. They want to help and mean well, but your four-star review translates into nearly the same bonus as someone's three-star review. Management training is another area that isn't highly invested in. It's just not seen as worthwhile as developing new projects and getting more deliverables out the door.

How does the dismal career advancement situation factor into the hiring process? Lack of solid career options within a company creates a desperate climate when those employees finally start their job hunt. Recruiter after recruiter comes across people who are in dire straits and need a new job immediately. If solid career advancement opportunities existed, the job seekers would naturally have more leverage than the hiring companies did. This isn't created by design; it's just an indirect benefit companies gain by ignoring the career pathing situation.

No Normalized Salaries

I mentioned how salaries are hidden. I've been in charge of peers where there was a $48,000 salary difference among people on the team doing the exact same work—and the lesser-paid individuals were much, much better at it. Whenever I would fight for them to get more money, it would always be based upon their current salary, not some objective number that a given position should make. "Oh, that analyst is making $62,000? Okay, let's bump them to $65,000. Their peer is making $122,000? Okay, let's bump that one to $128,000." There's never talk of normalizing the salaries across the groups. There's no standard for pay, just ranges. And if you happen to blurt out that you're making less than their range? They'll gladly undercut you.

To be fair, just like the lack of career advancement situation, the low-balling isn't necessarily malicious doing on part of the recruiters. They're given an overall budget for an entire department. If they can get three new hires for $210,000 total instead of two new hires for $210,000 total, they're going to get three new hires.

Inadequate Investment in Recruiting

Another area that sorely needs investment and innovation is the recruiting teams and methodologies themselves. Companies do not invest in their recruiting for the same reason they don't invest in career pathing or management training. It's just not seen as valuable for the return as doing something else with that money. The only innovation in years and years of recruiting has been online job boards like Monster or LinkedIn. While recruiting is still heavily a recommend-a-friend situation, individual job searching is finally starting to make a dent.

This may or may not be related to the "tech moving fast" situation, or perhaps the startup initiatives that came out of the late 1990s, but for whatever reason, tech companies in general never seem to even think about recruiting methodologies. The tools of recruiting haven't really changed in thirty years: word of mouth plus job boards. There have admittedly been an increase in the types and number of job boards, but this hasn't necessarily resulted in a net gain to the recruiting efforts. Applicants with poor networking skills have significantly benefited.

The Hiring Process Is Unrefined: Job Descriptions, Phone Screens, and Interviews

Job Descriptions Are Garbage

Don't get caught up in not matching a job description. When you get to see behind the curtain, you'll see that all the descriptions are slapped together last minute. People hate writing them and struggle to put anything meaningful together. Usually what happens is someone a long time ago made an okay posting, and the recruiters just slightly update it year after year. They won't have a real understanding of the technical parts of the job (or even an understanding of the non-technical parts!). If you're a "loose fit" or only match one-third of the terms on a job description, my strategy is to apply anyway. Always err on the side of applying instead of not applying. If it's a salary you want, or a job title in-name-only that you can leverage for your career future ("I'm a senior lead now!"), just fire away with that application. I still read job descriptions, but quite frankly it is easy enough to one-click apply nowadays that you're better off just ignoring the parts of the roles and responsibilities you think you're unqualified for and let the recruiters weed you out. Don't do their work for them! They're desperate!

Phone Screens Are Low Value, Yet Widely Used

The questions given to the recruiters aren't very well vetted, and it's typically not possible for the recruiter to meaningfully screen technical skill at this stage. As a result, they just talk to you and try to judge your character over the phone. If you seem like an okay employee, then they'll use your résumé as an example of your tech skills.

The second phone screen with the hiring manager is also not that relevant. He or she may have a list of three to five questions to ask. It will certainly be more technical than the initial phone screen, but again it's nowhere near a solid test of anyone's abilities. Because of this, almost all phone screeners heavily rely on their instinct and any rapport created during the phone screen itself. Which leads to two major problems:

They're Impersonal
By their very nature, phone interviews are impersonal. You're only one person on the interviewer's list of multiple people to call. They're likely running short on time, and they're using this call to find any reason possible not to call you on site for an in-person interview. Because it's all done by phone and is over so fast, you as the candidate don't get to let your personality shine, and the interviewer doesn't truly get a feel for who you are as a person and potential employee.

There's No Gauging Body Language
Regardless of how much preparation you've done, you might still stutter, make awkward sounds, or pause while you're thinking about how best to answer a question. In person it's easy for an interviewer to see from your body language that you're thinking of a response or that you've finished what you had to say. But over the phone, the only thing you're using is your voice, which is imperfect, so if you stutter or pause, the interviewer won't be totally clear on why.

Interviews Are Bad

Interviews are considered the most important part of the hiring process, and yet the way they're executed leads to meaningless or negative results. They're unstructured and the pass/fail of a candidate is almost entirely based on a gut feeling that the interviewer has. There are no standardized skill tests. Even developer coding exercises aren't run in actual job-like situations (e.g., "I would usually Google or Stack Exchange this" doesn't work at an interview). Interviews are also woefully short. You typically have thirty minutes to investigate the skillset of an individual that you would like to stay with your company for at least three years, hopefully many more.

From a validity or scientific perspective, interviews are an abysmal psychological tool for judging an individual. While there has been much written on this topic, detailing the specifics of the structural problems, I have a few of the major issues highlighted below. This will give you an peek into the issues that the recruiters, hiring managers, and interviewers are dealing with. Remember – they're unlikely to realize there's even an issue with the way they conduct interviews.

Interviews Cannot Measure Everything

How it is: Try as hard as you want, but you cannot measure technical skills, team skills, raw intelligence, someone's true attitude, or physical skills in a quick thirty to forty-five-minute question-and-answer session with someone. It's just not possible to be accurate here.

What works? As an interviewer, use work sample tests. It won't be great, but seeing someone in action is much better than just asking them about what they know. As an applicant, understand that your stories of your skills will be used to judge your actual skills. Highlight your complicated work, dive into details, and focus on the areas you contributed to, the problems you solved, the fires that you were there to put out.

No Scoring Sheets or Poor Scoring Sheets

How it is: The premise here is that since every team member asks different questions, it's impossible to combine the information from the director, the manager, and the coworker. Instead what ends up happening is the director, manager, and coworker just talk about their gut feeling. A scoring sheet would mitigate this problem of asking different questions, but quite frankly it has to be done incredibly well. Most of the companies I've been with never used a scoring sheet. Even worse, the ones that did had incredibly banal qualities that you were forced to rate and ended up not making any sense (e.g., Rate the applicant's ingenuity from a 1 to 5).

What works? If you're part of a team interviewing applicants, share your questions ahead of time with your co-interviewers. It'll level set what you're going to ask and they can ask similar questions so you have a comparison point. It's not perfect, but it'll help. If you're being interviewed, just know that there's really nothing you can do about this—it's an imperfect system, and if they even do use a score sheet, the scores are mostly based upon personality and how you come across in the interview. Do your best to be friendly and personable.

The Interview Premise Is Flawed

How it is: If you can take a step back and think about the interview dynamic, you can see how it's flawed from the start. The interview process is built upon this objective idea that all you have to do is ask questions and you can rate applicant one against applicant two with incredible accuracy. Hopefully you're as skeptical as I am of this premise. Even if you ignore the fact that applicants will exaggerate, possibly miscommunicate, or even flat out lie during an interview, you still have to contend with nervousness, interviewers asking terrible questions, the inability to compare applicant one with applicant two because they told completely different stories that don't really relate, and so on.

What works? As an interviewer, realize the limitations of the interview process. Ask the applicants to describe themselves working and try your damnedest to get a peek into their real day-to-day world. As an applicant, understand the game and acknowledge that your raw skills aren't under direct scrutiny here. Your communication ability, confidence, and friendliness carry much more weight.

The Plague of Confirmation Bias

How it is: First impressions matter for interviews, a lot. If you start out strong, the interviewer is more likely to continue to see you that way. A strong introduction, a timely but benign joke, a shared interest or bond that casually came up early on—any of these can have a heavy amount of influence and can lead the interviewer into simply confirming what their first-ten-seconds of instinct told them. Conversely, showing up late, being awkward, or simply not having "the vibe" the interviewer was expecting can lead them down a negative path of confirming that you weren't a fit from the start.

What works? As an interviewer, acknowledge the limitations of communication. Have some empathy, and understand that awkwardness or misunderstandings are bound to happen in a conversation. Additionally, give candidates the benefit of the doubt frequently. Rephrase your questions if you think they answered poorly. Realize that you might not be the best interviewer, or they may be incredibly nervous. As an applicant, try your hardest to start strong, and do your best to diffuse any strange situations that come up. You can't control their minds, so the next best thing is to try to convince them that you're friendly and enjoying the conversation. Additionally, just go on several interviews. If one in ten is awkward, then who cares? If one in two is awkward, you're going to be much more nervous about the outcome.

Interviews Aren't Predictive

How it is: This may be difficult to believe, but if you compare original interview results to an employee's actual performance, there's no predictive ability. Candidates who perform great on interviews may go on to be terrible employees. Awkward and mediocre interview candidates may easily go on to become all-star performers at a given job. It's very close to being completely random.

What works? As an interviewer, what's more predictive than asking a candidate some questions for thirty minutes? To put it bluntly, their past job performance. But isn't that what the interview is trying to establish? What was your past experience? Well, specifically, the biggest predictors are whether or not the candidate worked on difficult projects. Whether they volunteered or not is irrelevant—it's not the stepping up that matters, it's the fact that they executed difficult tasks. As a candidate, how do you use this to your advantage? I'll address this later in Chapter Ten, but it's always a good idea to do more than your literal job description. The more examples of specialty projects and working with cross-teams you have, the better. Even if employers aren't using scientific methods to analyze you, they'll still be impressed with your ability to get difficult work done.

Negotiation Sucks
Negotiations are terrible. They're usually last-minute on-the-phone conversations that take three minutes. They're also "closed door," which makes sense if you think of buying a car, but when jobs and careers are sold as great places to work for the rest of your life, it rings a bit disingenuous.

Companies Hire When They Are Desperate
This sounds like something normal, and if you think of the opposite it sounds completely alien—why would any company hire when they don't need the headcount? I'll get into that later (it's probably a good model worth trying), but as it stands, companies need help *immediately* whenever they are trying to fill a position. This creates pressure for them to solve their immediate problems. These factors can (and do) result in them accepting people after much less rigorous evaluations. I've been part of several conversations where the hiring managers have said, "Yeah, they're okay, not great, but I think they'll do the job and the team is hurting so let's hire them now." It's more about what effects this has on the process.

So that's the lay of the land. It's messy, it's not fair, and it's very random. But fear not, those factors are also what compelled me to write this guide. Counterintuitively, we can use this mess to our advantage. Simply being aware of it puts you at a big advantage over your peers. How? Let's dive in. Up next, the steps for getting that job!

Chapter Three:
Five Steps to a New Job

"In absence of clearly defined goals, we become strangely loyal to performing daily acts of trivia." — Unknown

So I've shown you what the tech scene is like. I've shown you how old your colleagues are, what the entry level salaries are. I've shown you the unfortunate situation that is recruiting in the tech industry. In this next chapter, I'll be detailing high-level steps and strategies for getting a new job based upon the current situation—from job hunting to phone screens to interviews, how difficult or easy it will be to get started, and also how tough it might be to keep going. The next few chapters in particular will specifically outline the flow to follow to get you from your current job to a better job with a more competitive salary. It's important to keep the entire process in the back of your mind as you're searching and communicating with recruiters, screeners, and interviewers. The negotiation setup starts the moment they initiate contact. Good luck.

Step One: The Résumé
I'll start with résumé building, enhancing the one-to-two pager you hopefully already have and how to keep it concise yet loaded with data to make it pop against the competition.

A critical note here is you do not have to be the best candidate for the job. You only have to be better than the candidates applying. It's a subtle point that's obvious after the fact, but very useful as an end-goal to focus on. Don't fret about looking perfect or trying to flawlessly execute each piece of conversation or email. One of the main parts of *Novice Negotiator*'s strategy is to pursue the job search in large enough volume so no individual mistake leaves you dead in the water. Things will go wrong. Events outside of your control as well as oversights on your end will occur. That alone is no cause for panic or alarm, because we're accounting for it by strength in numbers.

Step Two: The Job Search

This is the tedious part. It's important not to get discouraged at this stage. The reality is it will likely take three to six months for you to find a suitable job. That's okay, and you'll have to try on a regular basis. Once your résumé is in order, apply everywhere and anywhere you possibly can. Later I'll go into greater detail on how, but the general plan is to apply to about ten jobs per day until you've literally hit every possible job in the locales where you're willing to work.

At this point you'll start to get some emails and phone calls from recruiters. That's great, and I'd encourage you to engage nearly all of them. Just get yourself on their radar even if the specific job isn't an exact fit. Recruiters can have several job openings at any given time, and they will immediately contact you when a new opportunity opens up. Once you're in a recruiter's virtual Rolodex, they will email you every time there's the slightest chance you're a fit for a new job they just heard about.

Step Three: The Phone Screen

One way or another you'll get into the actual initial phone screen with an internal hiring manager or internal recruiter. It's going to vary from company to company, but either the external recruiter will hand you off to the internal HR recruiter, or they might pass you off directly to the internal hiring manager. The key here is to be friendly, confident, and appear flexible for negotiation purposes. Most companies don't phone screen hundreds of people per day. It's important to remember when you get this far that the people you are talking to are desperate for new hires. Their company is probably way overdue for a new hire and they just cannot find anyone. Don't undersell yourself, and don't bring up salary at this stage, ever. The time to talk numbers comes later.

If it does come up at this early stage, use some of the negotiation tactics I describe in Chapter Eight.

Step Four: The Interview

If you were friendly enough on the phone screen, they'll bring you in for a face-to-face interview. Again, it's important to just be personable here. As it turns out, judging someone's skillset simply by asking them questions for thirty minutes is incredibly difficult. Almost all of your interviewers will simply use their gut, whether they realize it or not. You can even have a stellar track record and some way to prove your technical or other job-appropriate skills, but if you give off a weird vibe in the interview, they will skip over you immediately. Don't worry—later on I have lists of questions you can ask to sound smart or be more personable.

Step Five: Negotiation

If the interview went well, your external and/or internal recruiters will begin negotiating with you. This is where the fun starts. They'll call you on the phone and get you to verbally confirm the offer before they send it over in writing. This is mainly because getting the actual written offers takes levels of approvals and can be a real pain in the neck for them if they have to go back to their boss or their boss's boss because they had the salary wrong. It also makes them look like they didn't have a good read on you. Regardless, you'll talk briefly on the phone and through a few emails before they send over the actual written offer.

Those are the five steps. They all might seem fairly straightforward, but I've learned that there's enough nuance to each step that I had to write a book about the process.

Everyone Is a Novice

This is important: when you're talking to the recruiters, it's quite natural to believe that they are experts. While it is certainly possible that you deal with an expert negotiator at some point, it is much more likely that you have someone else on the other end of the phone who also doesn't like their job, or perhaps isn't that invested in what's going on, or maybe just isn't bringing their A-game to the table.

The bottom line is: you're dealing with humans. If you put more effort into your job search than the recruiter does, you're much more likely to get a return on that time spent. Don't assume they know more than you simply because of their job title or how well they talk.

How to Use Unstructured Recruiting to Your Advantage

As mentioned above, a large part of these strategies is making yourself stand out in comparison to the other applicants. I would highly recommend getting involved with internal hiring processes at your current job (just interviewing prospective hires), so you can see the types of people you ideally compete against in the industry at large. If you're not in a position to actually interview new hires, at the very least ask other people on your teams what they think of each person they do interview.

Pay attention to how nervous they are, how sociable they are. You'll really get a good feel of where the bar is set in regards to who you have to compete against.

What Can Go Wrong?

Remember: almost everyone is nervous and stressed when they first begin the job hunt. Before you go through the process a handful of times, this is a perfectly reasonable reaction. As a result, several decisions in the multi-step process can be governed by fear—fear of never finding a "perfect" job, fear of losing your current job, fear of accepting a job only to hate it immediately. Recruiters will use this against you, either on purpose or just by the nature of their role. Be aware of it, and know that the best way to get past the nerves and fear is to simply apply and interview frequently. And know that many times interviewers are nervous or make mistakes too.

So that's our cheat sheet, from résumé to negotiation. Keep in mind that the strategies applied here are helpful for steering your career path. By applying to multiple jobs simultaneously, going on several phone screens, and interviewing at numerous places, your knowledge of the process and therefore your expectations will improve. The best way to get a taste of what's out there is to go out there! But we're getting ahead of ourselves. First thing's first, let's clean up that résumé.

How Long Will It Take?

In the US, here is the average time-to-hire for tech positions with at least thirty interview reviews:

Software Engineer: 35 days
Senior Applications Developer: 28.3 days
Product Engineer: 28.1 days
Implementation Specialist: 27.8 days
Hardware Engineer: 27.0 days
Quality Assurance: 25.9 days
Data Engineer: 25.8 days
Database Administrator: 25.5 days
Web Applications Developer: 23.5 days
Data Scientist: 23.2 days
Financial Software Developer: 19.9 days
User Experience Designer: 19.3 days
QA Engineer: 17.9 days
Junior Software Engineer: 15.7 days
iOS Developer: 14.1 days
.NET Developer: 14.0 days
QA Tester: 13.9 days
Java Developer: 12.5 days
Web Designer: 12.3 days
Data Entry: 8.5 days

https://research-content.glassdoor.com/app/uploads/sites/2/2015/06/GD_Report_3.pdf
http://www.itworld.com/article/2939497/careers/here-s-how-long-the-hiring-process-for-that-tech-job-will-take.html

Chapter Four:
The Résumé

"I don't understand this irony—valuable things like cars, gold, diamond are made up of hard materials, but most valuable things like money, contracts, and books are made up of soft paper." — Amit Kalantri

In this chapter, I'll be detailing the résumé, those few pages that summarize your entire business career. So much emphasis is placed on one's résumé that it's seen as the most important part of the job-hunting process. How do you get it right? How long should it be? One page? Two? Five? What parts are relevant, and what parts are a waste? When should you drop your education off? How do you know what to cut and what to keep? I'll walk you through each part. The good news is that despite all the weight put on this document, you don't have to get it perfect. Good enough will get you very far.

"A new survey of 2,200 hiring managers and human resource staffers by jobs website CareerBuilder shows that your résumé may get a bit more time before being cast aside. While some 17% of hiring managers said they spend 30 seconds or less, 68% said they scan a résumé for as long as two minutes before putting it aside. Still, that's hardly any time to impress someone who could determine your employment future."

"In fact, the study's eye tracking technology shows that recruiters spent about 6 seconds on their initial 'fit/no fit' decision."

http://cdn.theladders.net/static/images/basicSite/pdfs/TheLadders-EyeTracking-StudyC2.pdf
http://www.forbes.com/sites/susanadams/2014/03/17/the-best-and-worst-words-to-use-on-your-resume

---

Note that the above studies do not mean that they will only spend a few seconds reading your résumé, but that you have only a moment to hook them. If you succeed, they'll likely spend more time reading it and then hopefully contacting you.

What Counts?

Lots of people looking for jobs think that the résumé plays an enormous role in landing you a job. They'll spend hours or days crafting the perfect bullet points, cover letters, and introductions. "Is a large left border in bold purple better than a fancy logo of my own name?" Let's dial it down a step. Unless you're applying for a creative tech position, your résumé design is not something to stress over. Personally, I've gotten management-level jobs where no one even asked for my résumé during the entire process. While this is an extreme example, the truth is your résumé is vital for step one: getting past the recruiter. You're trying to look good on paper so they call you; you're trying to look better than the other résumés the recruiters have been staring at all day. Your résumé will not be the make-or-break of you getting the job, even though it can certainly feel that way. Again it really is just step one of this process: get that phone call/email/first point of contact.

The secondary goal of your résumé is for it to be a talking piece during the interview process. You'll use it to drive the conversation in a certain direction. Directly, you can steer things towards your résumé by referencing what's on it. Indirectly you steer things because those interviewing you won't have much else to go on besides what you've included.

Keep those two driving goals in mind when considering the following résumé-crafting tips.

Numbers!

One of the major failings of most of the résumés I've ever read is they are very generic when describing tasks, duties, and responsibilities. Bland and common words like "responsible for" or "worked on" are used everywhere but mean little. Instead, it's much more effective if you quantify your job tasks and duties with some type of number. Don't worry over the best way to do it or being exactly accurate. You're just using a different method to paint a much clearer picture.

Examples

Let's say you're a lead developer for a mid-sized company. You're responsible for managing a full team of six developers, and each month or so you have to hand off a mini-project.

How do we put that in bullet form on a résumé? How do we stand out from the sea of applicants?

Compare these two points:
- Lead Development Team and responsible for project delivery
- Lead Team of 6 developers; responsible for delivery of 2-3 projects each quarter

Both of these bullets may be saying the exact same thing, but most people write in a vague narrative form that matches the first bullet instead of the descriptive detailed form of the second one. When you say "Lead Development Team" instead of listing out the exact number of developers you lead, you're doing yourself a disservice. "Lead Development Team" sounds generic and dull, and also leaves recruiters with the question of how large of a team it was. Even worse, they may assume the size of the team you lead is smaller than their standard dev team. By explicitly detailing this, you accomplish two goals. First, you increase your chances of being more memorable than the competition. Second, and more importantly, if your exact number is close to or greater than the new job, they're more likely to think you're a fit. ("Oh, her dev team had six people? That's great, we only have four developers per team, so she'll be able to run our teams no problem.")

When adding numbers to your résumé, make sure to use exact detail on your bullet points. This is to set you way ahead of the pack. As mentioned above, most people use vague words like "assisted with improvements" instead of "improved performance by 23%." Even if they're describing the exact same situation, the 23% just sounds much better.

Examples of Quantifiable Bullet Point Details
- Less than 1% error rate
- Lead team of 6+
- Worked with 3 cross-regional teams
- Reduced {insert measurable problem} by 17%
- 30,000+ hour project
- Handled 12+ deploys per month

Be Concise!
Giving a lot of information clearly and in a few words; brief but comprehensive

Concise is the absolute perfect word for our résumé strategy. I can't state that enough. Give a lot of information clearly within a few bullets. Be brief, but don't leave anything absolutely vital out. You need to be painting a complete picture without spelling out every detail.

Don't List Every Detail or Even Every Job
Stagger the detail from most detailed to least detailed from job to job. Your most recent job should have the most bullet points. You want to give the appearance of growth. If your first job has ten

bullet points but your second job has three bullet points, it can look like you didn't pick up more responsibilities or just didn't do as much there.

For your most recent job, five to six bullet points is a good number, but it really will depend on the formatting of the entire résumé and your job history. If you received promotions or changes in job functions, make sure you list them out as if they are new jobs. You want to be very clear and call attention to any type of promotion, and separate listings are the best way to highlight this.

Don't be afraid to cut things from your really old jobs and simply bring them up in the interviews or phone screens if those details actually become relevant later.

Show Higher-Level Thinking
For whatever reason, an individual who shows initiative or can detail how they took on more than their individual job description will fare far better than someone who only stuck to their role, even if they executed it incredibly well. Paradoxically, managers want employees that manage themselves. If they see that you can run with projects without being hand-held, or that you saw a process need and fixed a problem on a grander scale, they'll generally see that as a bonus. Not having it certainly isn't a drawback, but if you can use any of the below tips, you will benefit.

- Think in terms of projects, either official company projects or long-term side projects you did yourself.

- Use words like "Built" or "Designed and implemented" to show you're not just plugging away and following direction, but also taking initiative.

- "Training" conveys that you have the ability to be a leader. If you've trained other people, you've clearly had to organize meetings, clarify information, answer questions, handle a group, and so on. This makes you valuable beyond just an individual contributor role.

- It'd be weird to load your résumé up with these, but an example or two looks good.

Word Choice

Vary your intro word on each bullet line. Don't just say "Responsible for …" twenty-two times down your résumé. The last thing you want to do is have the recruiter gloss over your bullet points. Avoid passive terms—"Experience in" is much worse than detailing what you actually did with the tech or skill you have experience in.

Your current job should be in present tense, while all other jobs should be in past tense ("Develop and maintain new framework" for your current job versus "Developed and maintained new framework" for a previous one).

Here's a list of options to spur your creativity for opening words: Accelerated, Achieved, Architected, Built, Centralized, Constructed, Converted, Created, Customized, Debugged, Delivered, Designed, Developed, Enhanced, Engineered, Executed, Expanded, Formalized, Founded, Implemented, Improved, Increased, Initiated, Integrated, Installed, Instituted, Launched, Led, Maintained, Maximized, Overhauled, Redesigned, Refined, Regulated, Remodeled, Repaired, Replaced, Restored, Restructured, Revitalized, Simplified, Solved, Standardized, Streamlined, Strengthened, Sustained, Transformed, Upgraded.

Use any that seem appropriate. Also, try to use specific examples or numbers after each word (Built 3 websites, Enhanced response time by 200ms, Improved process for 8+ Agile projects, etc.). Feel free to mix and match them as well. "Designed and implemented" go well together, as does "Instituted and led," and so on.

Skills Sections or Keywords
These are included because hiring managers will give the recruiters a list of words to search for or look for on a résumé. Typically include skills or tech buzzwords if you have several of them to list. I certainly wouldn't include a skills section if you only have three items to list. If you have a bevy of tech words then it can sometimes be beneficial. Be sure to Google them to get the most relevant terms, since the official buzzwords can change from year to year. Otherwise, simply try to incorporate them into your existing bullet points rather than in a standalone section.

Company Descriptions
Some résumés include a short description about each company to inform the reader what said company actually does, just in case they don't recognize the company in question. I never include these descriptions. As a rule the recruiter should either already recognize the company name because you're in the same industry, understand what the company does by the role you describe with your bullet points, or Google your company if it really matters.

Brief company descriptions just take up too much real estate on the résumé. And they can be completely irrelevant if the company's main focus is something that's not tech related at all (like clothing or grocery chains).

Formatting

Keep your résumé simple. Keep it focused. As a general rule, no bullet point should run more than two lines. You're not going to wow anyone with a lengthy narrative. Maintain a clean and clear résumé, and remember your audience—recruiters. Those recruiters will scan anything that hits their search results. Unless you're applying for a creative or UX job, they will not care how fancy of a font you've chosen—and that fancy magenta flower on the left margin can go as well.

Keep it simple
- At the top, center your name, email, and phone number (don't include an address, and don't worry about listing locations—it'll only serve to cut you out of the running if the recruiter assumes you live too far away from a job you otherwise would've had no problem commuting to), underscored with a horizontal line.
- List your jobs in reverse chronological order—current job to first job out of school. For each, list the company name, your job title, and the date range you worked there. Remember to be concise, quantify, and use direct, specific words in your bullet points describing your responsibilities. Underscore this section with a horizontal line.
- List your education at the bottom (unless you graduated in the past three years, in which case, put it at the top). Add any relevant classes, internships/co-ops, or honors if you don't have much work experience and need to fill up space.
- Don't bother with headers. People will understand that your jobs are "Work Experience" and that your schools are "Education" (although the education header is okay if you need to fill up space on your résumé, but it certainly is not required by any means).

Nobody Cares About Your First Job

Some people really fret and stress about each job on their résumés, and until you go through the experience several times and get a full picture of how little certain things matter, this is quite a normal reaction. However, the simple fact is that recruiters are barely reading your résumé, internal hiring managers are somewhat reading it, and both groups really only care about recent or relevant experience. That first job you got out of college is so far down the list that it doesn't matter.

My advice here is not to waste time trying to make it look good, as this could actually backfire if it looks like you took a step down when you moved to your second job. If your second job doesn't have as much detail as the first one, or if they just misinterpret the situation, it could look like you didn't progress at all in your career. As a rule of thumb, make your bullets points and descriptions grow in detail and importance as you move towards describing your current role.

Typos!

Recruiters do not have much to go on, so if they see any mistakes in your résumé they may simply discount you when comparing you against others. They need some sort of criteria to go on when choosing who to contact, so try to make it your details rather than a typo that would get you disqualified. For that matter, have a friend review your résumé, just to get a fresh pair of eyes on it. Who knows, maybe they'll catch those terrible grammatical errors that spellcheck can't.

Résumé Examples

Here are some example bullets. Feel free to borrow and tweak them to suit your own specific jobs.

Project Manager
- Managed global team of 20 for multi-vendor, 50,000+ hour project
- Migrated 3 vendors over the course of 9 months to new in-house platform, including migration of customer data and inventory
- Designed and maintained capacity planning strategy for 11+ projects over the course of 2 years

Quality Assurance Analyst
- Managed 20-60 bug fixes per two-week release with less than 1% error rate
- Tested proprietary SaaS Application and integrations with over 50 other third-party applications
- Streamlined automated regression process, increasing automated regression by 33%

Web Developer
- Created, improved, and maintained over 75 company websites
- Maintained and upgraded vendor web projects, delivering new features or fixes every 2 weeks
- Executed redesign for internal company website, collaborating with 4+ departments; responsible for mocks and finished deliverable

DevOps Engineer
- Single Point of Contact for escalations involving 3 cross-department systems
- Maintain and upkeep production monitoring of 400+ systems
- Design and implementation of continuous deployment system that verifies success, executes tests, and reports results on every successful developer commit

Tech Management
- Increased internal support efficiency year over year by 36% with 20% less bandwidth
- Managed team of 8, including career pathing, development of best practices, and day-to-day oversight on 5+ concurrent Agile projects
- Trended internal issues across team and reduced issues by 34% in key areas with long-term solutions

Chapter Five:
The Job Search

"Perseverance is failing nineteen times and succeeding the twentieth." — *Julie Andrews*

In this chapter, I'll be tackling the job search. What's the most effective method for searching for jobs? How often should you search? How do you handle the challenge of day-to-day searching?

Searching for a job can be daunting. There are so many options and avenues to pursue, how can you know which is a waste of time? It's very easy to get analysis-paralysis and simply sit and wait for a friend or colleague to recommend you come with them to their new job. Honestly, when that situation does come up, there's nothing wrong with taking it. However, if you want to increase your chances of finding a better job or being able to have options while you negotiate, it's going to require some fingers on the keyboard.

The main venues for job searching generally come from recruiters, job boards, and friends/colleagues. When it's time to apply, the core point is to get into a rhythm and apply often. Start at one application a day. Eventually you'll get into the groove and be able to hit three to five applications in a day.

Don't get caught up in the job description details too much. If the job is somewhat of a fit and you like the company or you're interested, just apply. They may not even contact you. Applying to jobs is so easy nowadays. Don't waste time up front by worrying as to whether or not you meet every single requirement before applying.

Remember: job descriptions are frequently incorrect. Internally they're copied from whatever was lying around, or perhaps were created by a hiring manager who doesn't have an in-depth view of the day-to-day. I've gotten jobs without five-plus years of experience in "required" fields or without knowing certain technologies and done just fine there. Don't negotiate against yourself; let the recruiter decide not to call you. Don't shy away from something just because there's a random bullet point on a job description you don't think you can hit. The company might not have ANY candidates at all so they'll take you even if you don't match their official list of skills.

The Scoop on Recruiters
Use recruiters and recruiting firms. In the early 2000s there was somewhat of a stigma towards using recruiters. People just didn't have a lot of information and assumed the recruiters were either scamming them or that you had to pay them to find you jobs. While this was (and possibly still is) the case for some people, the majority of recruiters these days do not require a fee to get you a job. Typically the recruiter will have an existing relationship with the company you're interested in. The way this works is only certain recruiters are "approved" for individual companies. The job-hunting firms work to fill several position for their partner companies, not just the job that may be a fit for you.

When you get to the point where you're negotiating your salary, don't factor in the recruiter's cut or pay. They may have to lose money on your specific hiring simply to keep the relationship in good standing with Company X, and then work to recoup their losses with another hire who comes in much lower than expected.

The earlier stigma against using recruiters has eroded greatly. Companies contract recruiter firms regularly to augment their existing recruiting department (which is usually only two to three people for a 200-person company). I would highly recommend using recruiting firms. Don't seek them out directly, but do speak with them if they reach out to you after you've applied to a company or two that they have a relationship with. Once this happens, they'll usually try to get you a job at any company they have relationships with if the first one you applied for doesn't work out.

Social Professionalism

You're going to meet and interact with dozens of people during your job search. When things don't work out with any given opportunity, never assume it is the last time you'll interact with anyone. Recruiters and HR representatives don't stay at the same companies forever, and they have new jobs all the time. Recruiters reaching back out for a second and new opportunity is a very real possibility (this has happened to me three times).

For this reason alone, it's best to be nice to everyone you work with. As someone who is skeptical of every adage, I find that the "Don't talk money, politics, or religion" one certainly applies at work. If you're not that outgoing, just do your best not to rock the boat while you're working. You never know which colleague you barely talked to will end up working at your next company. The acquaintances and random strangers you don't talk to on a daily basis could easily end up giving input to your future bosses.

LinkedIn

When LinkedIn debuted, it was heralded as the Facebook for professionals. It took a few years for it to take off and be seen as something truly established and worth anyone's time. However, as it stands today, it's not only incredibly likely that a well-developed LinkedIn network can land you a new job, but it could possibly be the best way to actually find jobs.

"Out of 100,000 profiles analyzed with BrandYourself, LinkedIn was the social network most often appearing at the top of results." - http://mashable.com/2012/08/02/higher-google-search-results

LinkedIn Strategies

As a strategy on LinkedIn, add absolutely everyone. The larger your network, the more recruiters will actually see you when they're searching. Add CEOs, add VPs, add anyone that appears important. If they don't want to add you back, that's okay. Most active LinkedIn users will simply connect in an attempt grow their own networks as well.

"Closer connections, such as a second-degree connection compared to a third-degree connection, improve your ranking in searches."
https://help.linkedin.com/app/answers/detail/a_id/50991/ft/eng

When searching for people to add, search for any given company and the word "recruiter"—this will get you all of the Comcast Recruiters, Google Recruiters, ESPN Recruiters, and so forth. If they're a company that's not just tech, make sure to try "tech recruiter" as well. Add everyone that comes up in the results. You don't have to even send them a message. Several will accept your add request and then contact you immediately. Even if they don't message you, it connects you to their network and you'll show up in more search results in general.

Connect with Everyone

You'll want to connect with just about anyone, but people who have large networks are more valuable as a rule since the reach of your connections is what determines how you show up in search results. It's six degrees of Kevin Bacon, but really only two and three times removed counts.

Apply Directly to Jobs

I highly recommend bulk-applying to jobs on Linkedin as well. Once your profile is up to date and matches your résumé, you can simply click-click-click and apply to several jobs at once. This plays well with our strategy to pursue several jobs at once. Most companies will allow you to apply directly with your profile, although some will take to you an external job site. Either way, applying through Linkedin is a great way to streamline and track your application progress.

Turn Off Publish Notifications

I would always recommend disabling the "publish notifications" feature. Otherwise, several of your current colleagues will see your activity and (perhaps rightfully) assume that you're looking for a new job. This can be disastrous. The other strategy to mitigate this is to simply update LinkedIn regularly—say, every week or month. If it's part of your routine, it won't be seen as out of the ordinary if your current employer were to look at your activity.

Beyond LinkedIn: Go Direct?

If you're not satisfied with just using LinkedIn or reaching out to former colleagues, you can apply directly on job boards or company sites (Indeed.com, ZipRecruiter, Monster, Careerbuilder, etc.). Fair warning—this can get a bit tedious. Likely you'll have to make a specific account for each company website if they're big enough. Don't expect a high return rate either. You may have to upload your résumé AND enter it in manually. Of course, if it works, it works. Note that whichever site you apply to will all funnel to the same HR department or recruiter dealing with that particular job opening. I recommend LinkedIn because of its ease of use, but you can find the jobs anywhere.

Cover Letters Too?

Several of these sites will have an option for you cover letter. Again, I would not recommend you upload a cover letter for a tech job. You want your strength to be in your résumé alone. A cover letter just lets them shortcut to skipping you after reading it. No one in tech is going to hire you based off a cover letter alone. They'll read it, then if they hate it they won't even look at your résumé. If they read the cover letter and like it, they can still hate your résumé. But if you only have a résumé, you avoid that possible pitfall and force them to just read your résumé. Avoid sabotaging yourself.

Know Your Competition

When applying for jobs the only direct competition here is another person applying to your exact same job. That's another reason not to sweat the process too much. If you feel your résumé isn't perfect, remember that it doesn't have to be. It just has to be good enough to get you to the next step. And remember, you're much more likely to get a job if you're one of the first to apply and interview for it. Apply to ten jobs a week just to test your résumé and phone screen skills. It will get easier and easier with each attempt. Get to the point where LinkedIn and the job boards are showing you the jobs that were posted in the last day. You'll be much further ahead and much more likely to have responses from active recruiters.

Chapter Six:
The Phone Screen

"The art of conversation is the art of hearing as well as of being heard." — William Hazlitt

In this chapter, I'll be walking through your phone screens—how to handle the preparation beforehand, the call itself, tips to maintain an appropriate demeanor, and so on. I talk about two types of phone screens here: the initial contact with an external recruiter (which is usually a quick five-minute call) and then the more in-depth fifteen- to thirty-minute phone screen with the internal hiring manager.

After your constant résumé uploading, job searching, and reaching out to all your trusted friends, eventually someone will contact you. Congratulations! You've moved on to the next phase. Don't stop applying, however—remember that one of the best tools that you and I have is strength in numbers. The more avenues for opportunity you maintain, the better your ability to negotiate when you do find a decent job.

The main advice for phone screens is to seem engaged over the phone. Remember, if they're calling you that means they picked you over someone else and already hope you'll work out. Just be friendly and talk to them. Your best strategy is to keep it light and ask one or two smart high-level questions. Don't go too deep in the weeds and don't worry about keeping it casual or not having enough questions. This is not the stage to negotiate salary or discuss specifics or sticking points. Instead act like you're very flexible and open on items like salary, travel, and job role.

Because the first phone screen is by an external recruiter, it might not even come close to accurately describing the job or work environment. You're really still trying to just get to the next step here. In a worst-case scenario, agree to everything the recruiter says over the phone, and then decline in email correspondence later when they bring up the next step. If the recruiter writes: "Just circling back. We had a great call and would like you to talk to Diane the hiring manager next!" To which you can then reply: "Sorry, I've taken another offer," or "I am no longer on the market." Why do this? Why not be upfront with the recruiter in the very first phone screen if you see a red flag? Because things change. Recruiters can be wrong. They might say the salary cap is absolutely $66,000, but after you get in the door they love you so much that of course they'll bump it to $71,000.

The only time I ever shut down phone screens right away is if they cold-call me and the position they're offering is so far down from where I'm at that there's no reasonable expectation they could match my salary numbers (for instance, they call about an entry-level position and you're looking for management tier).

Remember that if nothing else, any email correspondence that leads to you accepting a phone screen will provide you with good experience. Either it will lead to you getting a job, or it will give you a chance to practice your skills—how to respond to weird on-the-spot questions, trying out different ways to tell your career story, seeing what salary numbers they balk at. It's good to get practice in on that initial phone screen when you haven't yet invested much time.

Recruiters: Who Are They?
It's important to mention something newcomers to the job scene don't really consider: even though you might have applied on a company website, the person calling you about the job rarely works for the company itself. In the past ten to fifteen years, the tech recruiting and hiring model is to have a very light staff on site and to simply contract third-party recruiter firms as needed. As it stands, while Ms. Professional Recruiter might contact you on behalf of

ACME, she actually works for a recruiter firm that ACME has contracted out.

Why does this matter? For one, Ms. Professional Recruiter won't actually have firsthand knowledge of the work atmosphere. Any answers about the job should be taken with a grain of salt.

Secondly, it's likely that Ms. Professional Recruiter is actually more on your side than on that of the ACME Corporation. She probably gets paid on commission, or at the very least, makes more whenever she places an actual applicant for ACME.

You'll know right away if this is the situation described above if the recruiter starts referring to the company you applied to as "my client." In fact, if the recruiter found you on a job board, they'll likely not name the real company until the actual first phone screen. This is to protect themselves so you don't go apply to the job opening on your own or contact the company directly.

Recruiter Phone Screen Tips
Although some recruiters may call you directly, the initial contact will likely happen over email. (Hi I found you on/from so-and-so and think we may have a match. See the job here [link] and let me know if you have time for a phone call.) Here are some tips on how to handle the email back and forth.

- Don't respond immediately; let it wait at least a few hours. It's important to set the tone that you're not desperate. This will be critical later when doing the actual negotiation. They have to believe that you're a serious candidate who is pursuing multiple job offers, and all of this starts with your first interaction with them. Don't worry: if they reached out to you, it's because they haven't found anyone yet.

-   If you like the job in question but think you're unqualified, continue anyway. Remember that the job description may not be accurate, or they could be flexible on certain hard requirements. It's always worth it to spend fifteen minutes on the phone and find out more. Don't negotiate yourself out of a job; let the recruiters and hiring managers make that decision themselves. If they reach out to you for a lead role that you're interested in, it does you no favors to say, "I've never been a lead before, this sounds great!" or, "Well, I'm not sure if I'm qualified, but I'll give it a shot anyway." If you truly feel you're in over your head even at this early stage, you can politely decline in a follow-up email after the first phone screen. Remember: the initial information may not be accurate, so ride it out and learn more about the role.

A note about recruiter cold-calls on the phone: if they do reach out to you first on the phone, you don't have to answer on the spot. It's better to let it go to voicemail so you can listen at your convenience and get back to them instead. Otherwise you'll be randomly answering calls at work and constantly having to hide from your colleagues. I know people who do this—don't be one of them.

A Note About Salary
This is where things start. Don't bring up salary yourself; the recruiter will do that for you. It is common practice for them to be abrupt and forward about it. Towards the end of the brief initial screen, they'll say something like, "So what's your range?" or, "What is your salary now?" This is the recruiter establishing your

starting negotiation line. They won't tell you a range at first. Instead they'll start by asking you what your range is with the hopes that it's lower than the job's salary, which they initially keep secret.

It's important to practice this part, because as a general strategy you need to tell them the range you're expecting, not the true range you're actually at. For whatever reason, companies will only give you an additional few dollars based upon your existing salary. There's no industry guide that states that everyone in a certain developer position makes $67,000. You can be completely truthful, saying things like, "I'm at $46,000 but I believe my value is at $62,000." I've personally tried that route and can verify that this rarely works. The company believes you to be desperate as well, and will likely only offer you something like $51,000 if you go this route.

If you want to negotiate, you should pick a number that is realistic and is the true salary you would actually accept. Practice casually saying things like, "I'm currently in the low 100s," or, "I'm at $83,000 and change." If there's a discrepancy between the number you've told them you're at and their max number, just act flexible without giving specifics: "Sure, if the job's a fit, I'd be willing to move some, I'm flexible."

The recruiter phone screen is really to check three things: (1) are you alive, (2) do you think you match the job, and (3) are you within their pre-approved salary range. If you pass those three criteria, they'll move forward with getting you to the internal Hiring Manager immediately with the hopes that you're a fit. This typically takes a full week just to schedule. At this stage, they'll tell you the name of the company if they haven't already.

Hiring Manager Phone Screen Tips

Prepare, Prepare, Prepare!
I can't stress this enough. In the age of the internet, everyone should be able to research a prospective company. There's no excuse anymore. And yet, several people also vying for the exact same job won't even think about doing any research at all.

- Familiarize yourself with the job description, so you're not stalling and stammering if a specific piece comes up. Print it out and keep it handy during the actual screen.

- Google the company and see if there's any recent news about it. You don't need to bring it up, just be aware of it, and save it for the interview.

- If the screeners are part of the organization and not just a recruiter, view their LinkedIn profiles beforehand. Do this from incognito or a second account—don't tip them off to what you're doing, as you want them to be surprised and impressed in the moment when you wow them or come across as very professional or knowledgeable.

- Practice the questions and answers from the following **Questions They Will Ask You** section to get comfortable with them. Say them in front of a mirror. Say them aloud while you're commuting. You want to come across as very confident yet with a casual vibe.

Know Your Competition

Most people on phone screens are either brain-dead or not enthusiastic/personable enough. It's really hard to judge any type of skill over the phone, so it really is just a litmus test of whether or not you're a regular human being. How do you do better than the other people they're phone screening? Appear engaged and try to have a conversation with whoever's screening you. You might not have any questions or think the person screening you is dumb (at some point a dumb person will interview you, so get ready)—but from their perspective, if they have two candidates and one is engaged and talkative while the other is just saying, "Yeah, yes, mmm-hmm, nah, no questions," the engaging candidate is going to win out every time over the silent, awkward curmudgeon.

The Phone Screen Itself

- Know who you're speaking with (HR versus a technical person versus the person you'd be working for). Tailor your questions accordingly: ask HR people about the vibe of the place, if this is a new role or an existing one, if it's an existing one, why did someone leave, etc. Remember that this is just the initial screen, so don't plan on asking too many questions that would lead to in-depth answers. Save those questions for the on-site interview. I wouldn't start any debates on best practices or which technologies are better than others; only venture into a complex conversation if the Hiring Manager or whoever is talking to you starts it.

- While the initial screen will be quick, you should still take notes in advance and have them at the ready. Your notes should include whatever generic two or three questions you were going to ask, the names of the people on the phone screen (the first round is likely just the recruiter), the job title and company name (this will become more and more important to write down as you apply to more and more jobs), etc.

- Note that your phone screen could be multiple rounds, though most screens start off with just a hiring manager or recruiter talking to you.

- If it's multiple rounds/people, pace yourself and have some notes handy for what to talk about with each one. It's okay (and actually advantageous) to talk about some of the same general stuff each time so your screeners have the same point of reference when discussing whether or not to bring you in for an in-person interview.

Questions They Will Ask You
Below is a list of questions that the original phone screener will almost certainly ask you at some point. As a general rule, make sure you rehearse your answers and feel comfortable. The important piece here is to sound professional, somewhat casual, and friendly.

"Why are you looking?"
It's interesting to consider why they would even ask you this question. In a vacuum you'd assume that the recruiter wouldn't care about why you're looking for a job, right? If you're looking, then you're looking; why does it matter?

Obviously this question is code for another question. What they're really asking is: "Will you quit this new job too?" Specifically they're hoping you're a stable employee who's just looking for a good fit where you can work for years. "Why are you looking?" is a pretty transparent question when you realize what the recruiters are truly asking. Those who don't realize what the game is end up giving away more information than they know.

Good Answer: "I'm worried about my future at my current employer. Upper level management doesn't seem stable. They keep changing what my role is, and I've had four bosses in two years."

Bad Answer: "I'm bored at work. My job sucks. I don't like who I work with. I want more money. I want to be recognized."

The good answers here are any that convey two things: (1) you're not at fault for your current "bad job" situation, and (2) you just need a stable job where you can plug away and do good work. A bad answer would convey that you are unmotivated, prone to complaining or negativity, or high maintenance.

"Tell me a bit about yourself. What are you doing at your current job?"

Good Answer: Talk for fifteen to thirty seconds about your general work. Try to talk about things you really like and appear enthused.

Bad Answer: Anything that highlights problems or sounds like you're complaining ("Every day I do the same stuff").

The goal here is to appear like you're handling a solid workload, that you have a routine, and that you're a skilled individual. It's important to keep it somewhat brief as you don't want to drone on and on. Allow the screener to ask follow-up questions if they need more detail.

Since the above two questions will always have similar answers from phone screen to phone screen, feel free to write down a mini-speech if you need help. I find it easier to use bullet points and then just paraphrase the bullet points each time so it comes across more naturally.

"Why do you think you're a fit for our company/team/this job?"

Good Answer: "Company X seems really [forward thinking, on the cutting edge, fun yet challenging, or any other progressive adjectives/descriptors] and I really work well in that type of atmospheres." Keep in mind that they'll never contradict you with anything negative about the company. You can also include anything that highlights your ability to do good work without being rewarded: "I just need a place where I can focus and really get my work done, Company X sounds like a place where people get things done—more so than at my current job, that's for sure."

Bad Answer: Saying anything that's too generic about "being a hard worker" or something frivolous about how "the commute is great."

"Are you looking anywhere else?"

Good Answer: Yes.

Bad Answer: No.

This is a critical question to say yes to. To understand why, put yourself in the recruiter's shoes. Why would they care if you're looking elsewhere? Won't they just offer you a job regardless? Yes, but recruiters ask this because they're trying to size up their competition from the start. If you tell them you aren't looking anywhere else, it gives away a bit of your leverage. If the recruiter thinks they have competition, then they're much more likely to move faster and get back to you in a timely fashion.

This will help later when it comes to negotiating an offer. If the recruiters believe you have other options, they'll be more likely to increase your job offer. If they think they're the only game in town, then they'll be less likely to move quickly, and they might even not negotiate at all if they believe you're desperate enough.

"Do you have any questions for me?"

Good Answer: Yes.

Bad Answer: No.

It's vitally important that you have some questions for the screener, even if you already know the answers or don't actually care about the answers. It's important because you're trying to show interest and continue the dialogue. Getting the screener to talk a bit also improves how you come across.

"Yes, I have questions for you!"
Here is a list of questions that are appropriate for you to ask at this stage. This list isn't exhaustive, and feel free to ask specific questions based upon what comes up during the phone screen itself. I've put together what I think are generic questions that should work regardless of the job specifics, which is exactly what you want to be asking in the first round of the phone screens. To reiterate: a phone screen is designed to be brief, so don't go too in-depth on any of these. I would only follow up if there's something

very confusing that you care about in the moment. It's quite easy to get clarification or additional information later.

"What type of work is this role responsible for?"
Believe it or not, sometimes this question isn't covered by the recruiter when they first call about the job. They may just focus on the atmosphere or how great it will be to work at Company X. It also sets the stage that you're "considering" the role, not that it's a slam dunk. It flips the script a bit and reminds the screeners that they have to convince you to take the role, which helps create leverage later during actual negotiations.

"How's the work environment? What's the atmosphere like?"
The "work environment" and "atmosphere" are the most polite and subtle ways to ask them about the dangers of a job and whether or not it's a terrible place to work. Remember, they're desperate. They need to hire someone. You're probably the tenth person they're interviewing.

Great answers will be along the lines of, "It's laid back, people really respect your space and let you get your work done when you have to." Bad answers are trickier to identify. Just be cautious of anyone who says things like, "We work hard and play hard," or any answer that tries to convey, "It's very stressful but that's okay." This is certainly a question to ask everyone, and compare all the different feedback to get an accurate picture of what the office is like.

"How's the team I'd be working with?"
This question will also help you uncover any subtle red flags. Be cautious of any qualifiers such as, "It's a mixed bag but mostly the team is great!" Anyone who says the team is "just okay" or anything shy of "really good" is trying to tell you they don't enjoy their

coworkers. Social dynamics work against you here. Think about the other side of the table. It's actually quite awkward to tell a stranger that you don't like your coworkers, especially if that stranger ends up getting the job. The interviewer may not like the job themselves, but they can't give you an objective answer because you might take the job anyway and go tell Bobby that Sammy doesn't like him. Keep your ears open for any answer that's not, "Great, I love working with them," and you'll do fine.

"What do you (the screener) like best about working here?"
This is another question to ask several people throughout the process. Here we're just asking the screener, but make sure to continue to ask as you get to the next phone screen or the on-site interview. Just as before, mediocre answers are warning signs. If the best thing the screener can think of is, "It's close to my house," then you probably don't have an enjoyable job on your hands.

A lot of times, genuinely positive answers to the above questions can make you even more enthused about a job. It's important to get used to asking them frequently, especially for interviews at different companies. Once you've asked these a few times, you will immediately be able to recognize and differentiate between the amazing and awful answers.

"What are the next steps here?"
As you're wrapping up, ask for clear next steps and try to get a timeline: "Okay, sounds good to me, so what's phase two?" This is very important. What you're doing is setting up what phase two would be if the screener likes you after this short phone call. If your additional job searching hasn't come up yet, now is probably the last chance to insert it. When they mention, "I'll have to circle back with so-and-so, we should get back to you within a week," you can

reply, "That's actually great, because I have an in-person interview at Company Y next week too." It's important not to be vague here. Do your research and specifically name a large company in the area that the recruiter/HR rep or screener would know. Picking a large company is a good tactic because their size means they are likely always hiring and the recruiter would have no way of knowing otherwise.

Talking About Your Other Job Hunting

However it comes up, you'll eventually have to mention that you are, in fact, looking at multiple places for new jobs. The first time it comes up, you want to have that standard mix of professionalism and matter-of-fact casualness. If you truly do have another job prospect, feel free to share that, along with where you are in the process.

If you're willing to play the game, however, I suggest at a minimum selecting another company and mention that you are one step ahead of wherever you are at in the current process with Company X. This is a great way to set the schedule and cadence of updates. If they like you as a candidate, then you're already setting the expectation that they'll have to move somewhat quickly. If it's your first phone screen, mention that you have an on-site interview with Company Y soon. If you're at the on-site interview with Company X, casually mention that you have a second in-person interview with Company Y next week.

It's important that your comparison company in this example be not too far ahead in the process, because you want to be able to use them as leverage later. You might have to "wait for their offer" at some point—which wouldn't make sense if Company Y was too far ahead of Company X this entire time.

What NOT to Ask

- It's a phone screen, so don't go in depth with things. It's impossible to read body language over the phone and you won't have as good of a grasp as to how the conversation is going. Keep things light and casual. If during your Google searches you found something interesting about the company, save it for the interview so you can read their reaction in person and have more to talk about.

- Don't ask any complicated technical questions unless you and the screener are on a tangent that they started. Complicated conversations don't play out well over the phone because you can't read body language and at some point somebody's going to say "What? I didn't hear what you said," and just ruin whatever complex point you were trying to get across. High-level questions and theories are great, but don't ask them to explain their custom frameworks or anything that may have long answers.

Follow Up!
- As mentioned above, have a casual way of asking about phase two at the end of the call.

- After the screen, don't reach out first; use the timeline they hopefully gave you when you ended the call. If they're interested they will absolutely reach out. You're not going to "remind them." If they forget you then you didn't get it anyway. Reaching out only makes the recruiter think you're desperate to move and they will try to use it against you when negotiating.

- In the same notion, thank-you emails don't tip the scales and can sometimes seem like desperation instead of professionalism. I know there's some idea out there that psychologically you'll be more memorable than your competition if you send an interview thank-you note, but really it just makes you seem dated.

- If they pass on you after the screen, that's okay! You're connected to the recruiter and are already on their radar for future jobs. The main goal of applying to lots of jobs is obviously to get through to the interview process, but a secondary goal is connecting with all the people along the way so their future applicant-seeking endeavors include you.

Chapter Seven:
The Interview

"Confidence is a habit that can be developed by acting as if you already had the confidence you desire to have." — *Brian Tracy*

In this chapter, I'll be discussing the interview—how to prepare, what to bring, how to dress, what's a good demeanor to have, and how to handle it all without breaking a sweat.

Let's be clear: this is where you get or don't get the job. The pressure is on, but just remember that if you made it this far they're really interested in you and certainly selected you over other candidates. Most companies don't waste people's time when they can help it.

Pre-Interview, Post-Phone Screen

Before the interview, you've already had at least one phone screen (which we've covered in Chapter Six). Assuming it went well, the external tech recruiter will generally reach out to you by email and mention that their client would like to bring you in for an on-site interview. They may do this over the phone, but at some point you'll have an email confirmation.

The Next Email Correspondence!

"Hi Job Searcher, the phone screen went great. They'd like to bring you in for an on-site face-to-face. What's your schedule look like this week?"

It's again important not to reply immediately. You definitely want to respond with enough time so the recruiter can coordinate people's schedules, but there's no need to reply within the first 30 minutes. This plays into your long-term negotiation strategy. You're interested and this is a priority, but you're not desperately refreshing your inbox hoping they reach out to you. A solid move is to reply later in the evening to make it appear like you have a time during the day when you catch up on emails.

After you confirm the time, figure out a way to ask what to wear. It's very rare that you need to wear a suit or formal business wear anymore. As a general rule, business casual should be fine. You want to be one step above how you expect they dress in the office. Feel free to say something along the lines of, "I assume business casual is okay?" You don't want to appear helpless, and you certainly don't want to under/over dress.

Men: If the environment is one where men wear slacks and a button-down shirt, wear a suit and tie. For a more casual office where employees wear jeans and T-shirts, business casual (dress slacks and a button-down shirt) is appropriate.

Women: In the tech world, which is often laid back in its style of dress, it's smart for women to pick a tailored look for their interview. Try slacks and a dressy blouse, or a tailored skirt and blouse with a cardigan or lightweight sweater, and avoid big jewelry or dramatic makeup.

Requesting Fake Time Off

Once the schedule is confirmed, you'll likely have to request off at your current job. If they have a very lax working-from-home policy or you typically can give last-minute notice, obviously this won't be a problem. However, if taking time off is something that's incredibly formalized, here are a few suggestions besides the classic "I'm sick."

- Dentist appointment
- Possible jury duty (note that some companies require you to bring proof of this if you do go)
- Car trouble (this needs to be used day of)

- Court date (this one is typically very effective, as most people won't prod for more information since it could be an extremely personal reason like family court)

I've never been in the situation where time off was denied and I couldn't fake a sickness, but if you're truly stuck, try to work out an after-hours interview or a quick lunch interview if the place is close enough to your current office.

Prepare! (Again)

You have your interview date scheduled and confirmed, and you have your time off at your current job. Time to prep for the on-site interview. Take notes. You'll be doing this for several jobs. The first time you visit a company website you might think you have everything, but there's no need to skip note-taking, especially as writing things down often helps you remember them. Feel free to bring your notes with you to the interview.

Visit the Company Website
- Look at their "About Us" page.
- Read a few entries on their blog.
- Check their Twitter and other social media account(s) and read the most recent posts.

You're looking for anything interesting that might come up naturally in the interview process. The interviewer may say something like, "We have an annual retreat for everyone that's coming up in June." You'll look much better if you can casually say, "Right, I saw that on your blog, it looks fun."

Google the Company
- Skim the first few search results.
- See if there's any recent news (controversial or otherwise).

Similar to visiting their website, you're simply educating yourself with details that may or may not come up naturally in the interview process. It's important to be aware of any controversial news the prospective company has been involved in recently, if for no other reason than not bringing it up accidentally.

A quick note about Glassdoor and other sites that focus on "company reviews": Most are incredibly biased (in both directions) because of two reasons. First, people who are upset are motivated to rant and give a terrible review. If you had a great experience at your past job, you've likely just moved on to your new one and probably didn't even think of going online to crow about how great they were.

Secondly, and a bit more sinister, almost all of the company-review sites allow the individual companies themselves to remove negative reviews. This is probably to avoid any libel lawsuits. So take anything you read with a grain of salt.

Search the Interviewer(s)
- If they gave you a schedule of people you're meeting with, view their LinkedIn profiles from incognito or a second account just like you did before your phone screen. Don't tip them off that you're doing research ahead of time, you want to wow them on the spot.
- Take notes of what questions to ask each person based upon their role. Three questions each is fine.

Rehearse!
- Talk in front of a mirror, read through your résumé, and ask yourself: "Tell me about …" for each bullet point. Have something to say for each item.
- The goal here is so you're not caught off guard and ruin the cadence of the interview or look like you're making something up on the spot. It also gives you time in advance to practice and revise your answers so they sound really good.

Getting There
- **Dry-run**: If it's close, drive there from your house a day or two early so you're familiar with the drive ahead of time; if it's not close, look it up on Google Maps and walk yourself through the directions so you know how long the drive will take.

- **Get there early**: Aim to arrive thirty minutes beforehand, just to give yourself some time in case there's bad traffic or other unforeseen obstacles like parking. It's perfectly fine to enter the building fifteen minutes early, and I would recommend using the facilities on site before you actually check in with the receptionist for your interview (or tell them you're there, but ask to use the restroom first).

- **Eat beforehand**: You might be there long enough that they provide you lunch, but I wouldn't count on it. If you've learned anything thus far, it's that you can't expect the interview experience to necessarily be professional; there might not be one appointed person in charge of chaperoning you. I've been on several five-plus-hour interviews where no lunch or bathroom breaks were given.

Know Your Competition

Most people are really damn nervous during interviews and just have nothing to say, so any stories you have or questions you ask will go far. Remember you're not trying to beat some imaginary objective test. You're trying to beat the other schmuck who interviewed last Tuesday that they don't like. If they're interested in you at all, it'll either be because you're one of the first people and they need help ASAP, or you'll be the unicorn they've been waiting for and can end the millions of interviews they've already done.

The Interview Itself

- Keep in mind that the people doing the recruiting will have an outdated job description, probably the wrong idea about the job, and that the people interviewing you may have just been grabbed a minute before or not even know why you're here. Make sure you bring your notes!
- Group or one-on-one? In my personal experience, there's about a 50% chance of there being multiple interviewers at the same time. Don't fret! All this advice applies to both situations. With multiple people, you just have more opportunities to get everyone else to talk.

Questions They Will Definitely Ask You: The On-Site Interview

"Tell us about yourself."

Good Answer: "I've been doing [relevant field to the job] for X years, most recently at Company Y and before that at Company Z. I'm comfortable doing [job function A] or [job function B] or even [cutting-edge new technology or something up and coming]."

Continue into your actual job experience for a bit, but keep the entire answer brief and to forty-five seconds to a minute tops. This is your opener. You just need a sky-high elevator pitch, you don't need super detail here. Let them press for detail with follow-up questions.

Bad Answer: "I really love cooking shows, hanging out, and binge-watching Netflix."

Avoid personal answers. They may come up naturally in the conversation, but certainly don't lead the conversation with your personal likes and dislikes. Steer the conversation to your professional experience and the projects or great on-the-job stories you want to talk about.

"Tell me about your day-to-day routine."

Good Answer: "Typically I start by checking emails or texts on my phone to see if there are any emergencies before I get to the office. Once nobody needs my help, I get started on my to-do list, and will likely spend an average day [performing job function relevant to your NEW job] along with [other job function that's likely very relevant to your new job]."

Frankly, this is a great time to pour on the details. I would even give them a literal example of what you did last Tuesday. Pick your busiest day where you also managed to accomplish a lot (busy not because of meetings, but because you got a lot done). The point here is to illustrate how you can multitask and handle stressful scenarios, without being explicit about the fact that that's what you're doing.

Bad Answer: "Well, I do a lot of stuff. I roll in around 9:15 or 9:30, and kinda just do whatever until my boss shows up. Everybody's real relaxed. We go to lunch at like 11 sometimes."

Any answer that paints you as lazy and unmotivated or is really vague and just makes it seems like you're in meetings all day or just responding to emails or waiting around to be told what to do is bad. You want to look proactive, not reactive. And most importantly, you want to highlight the areas where you may already be performing this new job's function. You will be a much more attractive hire if they think you're already doing the job.

"Tell us about a difficult project or deadline or a tough/stressful situation."

Good Answer: "There was a project that was pretty important, so we were working around the clock and even a few weekends as we got closer and closer to the launch date. Four weeks from launch a misinterpreted but absolutely necessary requirement was found. It was going to push us back at least eight more weeks. Now, I'm not in charge of anybody officially over there but I immediately began reaching out and scrambling to put together emergency meetings for alternate solutions. We didn't hit the original launch date, but we managed to mitigate the delay by only three weeks instead of the possible full eight-week delay."

The above story is really vague. In your actual answer, be sure to dive into specifics. What I've crafted here is what you want to use for framing your detailed story. Talk about some really tough emergency or five-alarm fire that your group or team was hit with, and how everybody (including you) scrambled to get fix things immediately.

Be careful here. They're looking to see how you would handle challenges, so it's very important not to give some softball answer where you say something like, "Everybody thought we were screwed, but then I saved them all and there were no problems." It's much better to recount a story where things didn't go exactly right. Any situation where bad things happened and you had to have real tough discussions about how compromises were going to have to be made and couldn't totally solve the issue are much more indicative of your resolve.

Bad Answer: "Sometimes I had to stay late to get my work done. And one time I worked on a weekend," or, "One time my boss told me not to leave until I got something done." Another bad answer: "There was this project that had a TERRIBLE project manager..."

Avoid stories that are minor inconveniences. There's no strength in dealing with a situation that is only mildly bothersome. There's no point in holding back here. Tell your best story.

I've included the last example to highlight something important: Don't malign your old colleagues. Ever. Find creative and unique wording like, "They were interesting to work with sometimes," or, "Not everybody always got along, but we sure did get the job done." It's possible that you could be seen as complaining. It's damaging and dangerous for the interviewer to think you don't have a good attitude and don't play well with others—it could keep you from getting hired.

"What's your biggest strength and your biggest weakness?"

Good Answer: "My biggest strength … hmm …" (appear to be thinking on the spot). "My biggest strengths, or at least the ones I can think of, are probably how much I just love coming to work and really accomplishing something. Working with a team, contributing. It's kinda corny maybe but I don't really have another way to put it, I just really care about quality work."

"My biggest weakness … that's tough too. I'd probably say sometimes I struggle with opening up on a personal level. Sometimes it can take me a while to be the one going to all the happy hours with my coworkers. I gotta come out of my shell first, so maybe I might seem a bit guarded."

This is a terrible question. I hate this question. There are some strategies to answering this question where your weakness is actually a strength in disguise. Don't do this. I know I talk about how poorly designed a lot of this process is in this book, but it's actually incredibly awkward to be called out on the spot. If you answered that way and they say, "That isn't really a weakness," then you're taking a double hit. One because you are now the type of person who will dodge a question (in their eyes), and two because you have to answer the question again!

My strategy for discussing a weakness is to make sure it can in no way be related to your work. I usually default to a minor social flaw simply because it counts as a weakness and you get major points for revealing something genuine. Nobody will follow up or question your minor social flaw because that's incredibly personal and awkward, thus ending this question on the spot.

Bad Answer: "I'm not sure I'm a complete match for this job, my [insert skill x] isn't really where I'd like it to be."

As you can see, any bad answer here is one that puts additional doubts in their mind. Don't do their work for them. Maybe the interviewer wasn't even THINKING about your technical skills, and now you just made them front and center.

"Do you work better alone or in a team?"

Good Answer: "I can't really say which is 'better'—I don't really have a preference. It's great to collaborate with other people and produce great products, but I also really like to focus sometimes and crank out quality work. Either's fine, they're just different flavors."

This is really a non-question, so the strategy here is to somewhat sidestep it. The bottom line is there's lots of nuance to teamwork and individual contributor work. Maybe you work great in teams but it won't translate to the type of teams this new company has. Maybe you did great individual contributor work but at Company X it turns out that they would consider that team work because there were a few meetings about it. It's just not a valid question that leads anywhere, so the best advice is to bounce it back with a middle-ground answer that shows you're flexible.

Bad Answer: "I fly solo," or "Teamwork or bust."

Because you won't have any context as to what the interviewer considers a team or teamwork (collaborating daily? Touching base once a week? Just being assigned to the same project?), it's dangerous to give a straight answer on your interpretation of what they mean. You could ask them to clarify, but I don't believe that will translate well. Asking for clarification on such a "simple" question might immediately get you negative points.

"What are your thoughts on [industry standard x]?"

Good Answer: Whether this is Agile, or Microservices Architecture, Machine Learning, Continuous Delivery, BlackBox Testing, Automation Testing, etc., the best way to answer these is to describe something's pros and cons. "I see Agile as a toolbox, I don't use the entire thing as is, but rather adopt the pieces that fit for any given situation."

Bad Answer: Any short answer that shows no thought. "I don't know, I never thought about it," isn't good. Do your best to pivot into an area that you have thought about if you actually have zero experience or never heard of what they mentioned.

"Where do you see yourself in five years?"

Good Answer: "Well, let's say this interview works out and we both think there's a fit here. I'd like to get in, get my hands dirty, figure out some immediate and some longer-term solutions for [Problem X, Problem Y, any problem the interviewer has already mentioned]. A year or two down the road, hopefully I continue to provide value and can move on to [next level up, lead, senior, or even just saying "a role with more responsibility"]."

Bad Answer: "I don't know," or, "What's the career path here?" or, "I don't really know what my options are."

Those answers or any answer that says, "Probably doing the same job" is bad. The way to look your best here is to highlight your ambition in conjunction with your ability to provide value. Showing them you'd like to climb the ladder is great—but don't try to go TOO high up, just express how you certainly wouldn't be doing the same job five years later.

"Goofy Thought Experiment"

The Egg Drop Problem
You are given two eggs, and access to a 100-story building. Both eggs are identical. The aim is to find out the highest floor from which an egg can be dropped out of a window without breaking. If an egg is dropped and does not break, it is undamaged and can be dropped again. If an egg breaks when dropped from floor N, then it would also have broken from any floor above that. If an egg survives a fall, then it will survive any fall shorter than that. The question is: What strategy should you adopt to minimize the number egg drops it takes to find the solution? (And what is the worst case for the number of drops it will take?).

Fish Problem
Out of 200 fish in an aquarium, 99% are red. How many red fishes must be removed in order to reduce to 98%?

Three Light Bulbs Problem
Suppose that you are standing in a hallway next to three light switches, which are all off. There is another room down the hallway, where there are three incandescent light bulbs, and each is operated by one of the switches in the hallway. Because the light bulbs are in another room, you cannot see them. How would you

figure out which switch operates which light bulb, if you can only go into the room with the light bulbs once?

Generic Brain Teaser
Why are sewer covers shaped like circles? How many diapers does the US go through in a day?

Good/Bad Answer: Here's the problem with these goofy thought experiment questions: they don't work. Google started a trend a long time ago asking these brain teasers to "see how people think," assuming that it led to great hires. It sounds plausible, right? People who can solve tricky puzzles and have a tech background MUST be good at their job, right?

Unfortunately, no, there's literally no correlation whatsoever with getting any of these fancy riddles correct and performing well on the job. Google stopped using them around 2010. Just as unfortunately, not everybody got that part of the memo. Older individuals or people in certain circles will have a tricky "ace in the hole" question that they always use.

The best thing to do for each of these questions is to talk aloud about your thought process. Some don't have actual answers. Some do (if sewer covers were literally any other shape, they could turn and fall in on themselves, hurting any workers below). The answers are irrelevant. The best way you can be prepared is to APPEAR prepared when asked. If you're just dumbfounded and start sweating, that's the worst response. Talk through it, do your best, laugh a little, and fingers crossed they've gotten with the times and just don't ask one of these.

Questions You Should Definitely Ask Them

The most important part of this strategy is to get your interviewer to talk. Don't worry, it won't take much prodding. Most people don't feel listened to on a day-to-day basis; ask them questions about their current problems and challenges. A good way to frame these questions is that you're "taking a pulse" of the work environment. You just want to understand the vibe of the place, and you have some generic questions that you ask everybody (try to be casual about it).

"Can you describe a typical day-to-day for this role?"

This is important so you can flesh out exactly what you'll be doing, but it's also a great filler question because it takes a while for them to answer. Usually they won't have a great idea of the day-to-day activities anyway, but you'll get to hear them talk a bit more and get bonus points for asking what sounds like a great question. If they've already described SOME of the activities, just act like it's "on your list" and ask it anyway with the caveat of, "Anything else other than what you already described?"

"What's the biggest issue your team faces?"

This is an easy opener and gets them talking. Try to finish their sentences or rephrase what they're saying to show you understand what they're talking about. "Oh yeah, I know what you mean, we had a tough problem with bandwidth and too many projects at my last job too." But don't step on their answers and just try to let them talk as much as they want.

"Is there high turnover here?"

This is a question that could potentially uncover red flags, but truthfully what you're doing is reminding the interviewer that they have to win YOU over, not the other way around. It's subtle, and this question alone won't accomplish that task, but the moment they're trying to convince you to work there you'll have the job in the bag.

"What's the best part and worst part about working here?"
This is another one that might help you sniff out problems jobs, and it could if you're lucky. More often than not though, this is just to get the interviewer to open up a bit and start talking in a less structured manner. One of the reasons you are politely getting them to talk about their problems is there's a higher chance that you'll bond in thirty minutes if they're talking to you about issues and you have a sympathetic ear. Remember, when they leave, they're just judging you on a gut feeling.

"How does this company compare to YOUR last job?"
Preface this question by asking where they worked beforehand. It's another comparison question that sounds like you'll get good information from, but remember: Asking three to four people their individual opinions about something is incredibly subjective. This and the questions before it are much more useful as a conversational tool where you can safely get the interviewer to open up and talk about their life experiences instead of yours.

A quick point: the questions I've provided here are of course in addition to any legitimate questions you may have about the actual job duties.

Stories!
So I've given you some questions to ask and some questions to be prepared for, but for true success you want your interview to be more than just a simple Q&A session. Take a look at you résumé. You're going to use it as a guide. The interviewer will likely have it in

front of them as they're talking (and be sure to bring copies to hand out!), and this is your opportunity to tie a narrative to the paper profile you've created.

Expanding on the bullet points from said résumé, you should have two to three good stories that really highlight your work ethic, problem solving skills, and ability to work with others under stress. Throughout the interview, feel free to reference these at a high level. Don't get repetitive, but certainly go in depth once or twice per individual story.

Don't lead with any of your stories. You don't want to go in depth at the very start. You want to ping-pong a bit first. They'll say, "Tell me about yourself," and you'll say a few words, then they'll have a question or two. After this opening back and forth, feel free to begin to talk about that time you were working late and the power went out but you figured out how to get everything for the deadline done even though you didn't have a computer.

Stories are good for a few reasons. First, the conversational nature will make you appear naturally more down-to-earth and human. Secondly, remember that everyone who interviews you will touch base afterwards and share feedback. If they have nothing in common to talk about, then the feedback can be vague. If a certain interviewer didn't like you generally, it's tough for those who did like you to argue for your case if there's no common ground. When you share the story about how you saved a puppy from a fire, all the interviewers afterwards can talk and share their input. This can lead to them feeling similarly about you and overall it will simply generally increase your perceived value.

Do Not Do's

Don't talk salary ever (unless they bring it up). This is because you don't want to shut yourself out of a cap they may have up front. If the lowest amount you're willing to accept is above their range for a certain position, then there is little chance they'll even bother talking to you unless they're much more desperate than usual. Also, after you've met and interviewed and charmed everyone at your potential new job, they'll be far more willing to talk to people higher up the chain and try to get your salary requirements approved. No way are they going to try to do that without even talking to you first. If they DO bring up salary in person, make sure you're ready with all the advice from Chapter Eight.

Generally, I avoid personal questions only because it can lead into awkward conversations that can get the interviewer or yourself in trouble. There's something to be said about wanting to learn about your co-workers, but it's just too risky. The conversation could accidentally wander into something about religion or politics. There's not even a guarantee how much you'd be interacting with these specific three to four interviewers on a daily basis anyway. Don't take the chance.

Feedback, Leaving, and Setting Up Next Steps

- As you leave, make sure you say the usual pleasantries ("Nice meeting you," "Appreciate your time," "Good to talk to you, thanks," etc.). In addition, ask for a timeline casually from whoever your liaison on-site is ("Great, so what do the next steps look like?").

- If you can, mention something about an interview or follow-up interview with another place (Comcast, or any place that's big) in the following week. Just be casual and appear to be actively looking. The idea here is to put some pressure on them to act quickly. ("So you'll get back to me sometime in the next two weeks? I have a follow-up with Comcast next Tuesday so that works out.")

- Don't say anything directly negative about the process to anyone internal. If the hiring manager asks, "So how did it go?" don't say anything like, "That John guy who interviewed me was really strange." It'll only hurt your chances of getting an offer. It's quite possible the rest of the company knows that John is indeed strange, but it's also possible that they like him very much and it'll backfire. You can always decline the job later if "strange John" is weird enough to be a deal-breaker.

- Conversely, don't say anything incredibly positive. You don't want to tip your hand. It's perfectly normal to be polite and say things about how much you liked everyone or that the place is really nice or that you feel like you'd get along with everyone at the job, but there's no need to gush about how much you love this place if you really do think it's your dream job. It'll hurt the negotiations later if they know how desperate you are.

Follow Up!
- Don't reach out first; we're getting close to the negotiation stage. If they really want you, they'll reach out first. Again, there's no "reminding" or "convincing" that any follow-up email can do. The same logic from earlier that applies to thank-you emails applies here as well—don't send them. There is a much higher chance you'll come off as either desperate or creepy.

- If they do reach out, they will certainly start with a salary talk. The follow-up here is essentially all of Chapter Eight: Negotiation.

Chapter Eight:
The Negotiation

"Let us never negotiate out of fear. But let us never fear to negotiate." — John F. Kennedy

In this chapter, I'll be tackling negotiation and its challenges—what to do, how to do it, and the best strategies to use while negotiating.

By this point, you've made it. They've extended an offer. Great news! It's been a long ride—the résumé editing, the job searching, the phone screens, the interviews ... But don't accept that new job just yet. There's still a bit more, and it's important to keep a cool head.

Remember, while you don't explicitly negotiate salary in the very beginning, the strategy of this entire job-searching process has been set up to help you negotiate in the end. Your résumé makes you stand out from the crowds, you've been friendly on the phone screens and during the interviews, and this new company likes you and believes you to be somewhat flexible.

I'll be covering negotiation preparation, the verbal offer, and the counter offer in this chapter.

Negotiation Preparation
There are two important steps in the negotiation process. First, keep the communication going and try to avoid dead ends. The second is to have a casual vibe the entire time. You want to appear as if what you're asking for is normal and reasonable, which will make it much harder for them to disagree. Think about and practice the strategy I lay out in order to get comfortable speaking on your own behalf.

Talking Salary
Since before the job search, you need to have a clear goal number in your head. Normally the external recruiter already asked you this during that initial phone screen (refer to our chapter on phone

screens for how to handle the first time they ask what your salary is). Once you have that target amount in your head, the next step is to act like it's your current salary. For whatever reason, companies will refuse to give you a large increase, but they will always be much more willing to "make a slight bump or lateral move" instead. Internally they will ask, "What is he or she at right now?" when trying to figure out if they can bring you on board.

There are no standard salaries except for government agencies and very large corporations that have large Human Resources departments. Every other company you deal with will be flexible and have somewhat of a range. While there are numerous websites that purport to track salaries, the best way to gauge salaries for your job is to search for them in job search engines. Do this instead of using Glassdoor or other salary sites. Just add a dollar value to your job search and see what comes up, or look at the results and sort by salary range if possible (Indeed.com is great for this). For example: "Software Developer 75k" or "Project Manager 115k" or "Sr Business Analyst 92k." It's much better to use live data that's out there for immediate opportunities anyway.

Rehearse!
As mentioned above, companies are more willing to match your current salary than give you a giant bump. It's an unfortunate truth of the situation. For whatever reason, they simply balk at giving you more than a 3–5% increase. To combat this, have your goal salary in mind and state it as your existing salary. This requires practice. Make sure you practice saying your new salary, including the actual phrases you're going to use. (For example: "I'm at X and anything comparable or slightly higher would be fine.") It's important to sound natural and confident during the exchanges with the recruiters. It can also be helpful to go back one or two jobs and

write down what your inflated salaries would've been at those older jobs. Sometimes a recruiter may ask for your full salary history.

The more natural and casual you sound about your inflated existing salary, the more likely they're willing to accept that that's your true number. I can't stress this enough. For whatever reason, internal salary discussions always revolve around where the person is at currently. Instead of a company paying all developers $70,000, they'll try to find out if a newly hired developer is below that minimum range. If so, they'll give that person a slight bump over their existing salary—say, bumping them from $60,000 to $62,000. Companies are trying to save money and are operating under the assumption that new hires are happy with any pay increase at all.

It's not actually possible for the new company to verify your salary in any way. Unless you're in a government job or at some very large company that has published salary standards, it's your word versus the recruiter's.

The Verbal Offer

If one of your many job interviews is successful enough, the external recruiter will reach out a few days later, most likely over the phone. This initial negotiation outreach is rarely handled in email. They like to somewhat ambush you and hopefully convince you to take the initial offer. At the very least the recruiter will be feeling you out to see if their range is acceptable.

How is this done? Oddly enough they don't write up the offer and send it over officially until they're absolutely sure you're going to accept. Why, you may ask? Think about the perspective from the recruiter side. Ms. Professional Recruiter can't just make up whatever offer she wants. It has to be approved by your future bosses at the ACME Corporation—usually at least two levels of managers or executives.

Ms. Professional Recruiter's reputation and relationship with ACME Co. is on the line here. If she goes through all the red tape to get you an official offer from ACME that you then rejected, it would look like she couldn't do her job and didn't have a good read on you as an applicant. Additionally, no one wants to go through multiple rounds of approval in the first place. It can take weeks. Doing it more than once? That's asking for trouble.

As a result, Ms. Professional Recruiter will call you on the phone at some point after your great interview and say something along the lines of, "I think we have a fit here. Everyone liked you. They're willing to make an offer." The recruiter will either sound very enthusiastic about the offer or have a cool professional tone that's meant to say "This offer is great and speaks for itself." Either way, it's time to start negotiating.

Phase One: Politely Stalling
Regardless of the offer, you're going to "have to think about it for a bit" or "have to talk it over with the family first" or any other reason to not agree on the spot. This is for your benefit. You want to spend the time mulling over the offer on your own, without the recruiter's ability to read your response. This will also set you up for a level-headed counteroffer as part of a new conversation. You don't want the recruiter to have a solid read on that either.

How do you stall on the phone? First, make sure you sound medium-interested, even medium-to-highly interested in the offer if it is indeed close to what you'd be willing to accept in your head.

Don't be negative about it—you need them to realize there's an active path here where you'll likely accept the job. This will set up your requests to be seen as small obstacles since they will more likely feel close to the deal. Otherwise, any of your counteroffers could be seen as the last straw if the recruiter just flat out didn't think there was a chance you'd accept.

The second part of stalling is to begin asking about somewhat relevant job details. Dovetail your conversation into things like, "What's the healthcare like? Fairly standard, I assume?" or, "What would the start date be?" or talk about paid time off, for example. Don't discuss salary here—that's the main negotiation item and we'll dive into that shortly, so only mention some incidentals. This is just to naturally extend the conversation and give you more time to come across as fairly interested. The alternative answer is to abruptly end the phone call, which of course isn't what we're looking for.

Phase Two: The Counteroffer
Always counteroffer. Always. They've come this far—they've looked at countless résumés, they've phone screened so many people, they brought in candidates for interviews. If they extended an offer, that means they chose you. There's no need to fear them canceling or retracting the offer. At worst they'll say, "We can't move at all, sorry," and you can just accept the offer that's already at your target level.

Timing

Once you have an offer from a company, they are READY to move. All the internal approvals have happened. More importantly, because no one wants to look like an idiot, the hiring manager has very explicitly asked the recruiter, "Are you sure this is the number we can get them for?" The hiring manager, the recruiter, and everyone who was involved in lining up your approvals will look like they don't know how to do their jobs if you turn down the offer. This is one of the major reasons why you have leverage at all.

Unlike other communications, I typically wait only about an hour or so before countering. The main reason is that on the other end of the phone, you know that all the right people are working that day. The recruiter will reach out to you the MOMENT they have all the approvals, so if they had to go back and adjust the offer by a bit, they can most likely get it done immediately.

Additionally, the recruiter may have been told, "Okay, so offer $57,000, but the ceiling is $65,000"—in which case your counteroffer could be accepted even faster.

How to Counteroffer

There are two scenarios: the offer is above your target level, or the offer is below your target level. Both are quick. You won't be going round and round on this at all.

If the original offer is below your acceptable level, then countering is easy. You call them back and say, "I really like the company, the people there seem great, and it sounds like the work I'd be doing would be very rewarding; but at this stage of my career, I just can't take that much of a pay cut. The lowest I could accept would be {insert the actual minimum salary that you would take}."

If the original offer is above your actual minimum salary requirement then it's still prudent to counteroffer, but just try to get them to move the needle ever so slightly. Unless the original offer is sky-high, there's no reason to immediately accept. Instead, politely stall as described above and then when you call them back, say something along the lines of, "I'm really happy with the offer, but if there's any way to bump the base salary, even slightly, or maybe if there's some sort of sign-on scenario, I'll be ecstatic. I don't want to play games, and if that truly is the ceiling, then I get it. But if there's any room at all, then I'd be over the moon."

They might call you out and say, "Well, how much higher?" If this is the case, then ask for whatever seems "small" relative to the offer: for example, $2,000–$3,000 on top of $85,000; $4,000–$6,000 on top of $120,000.

There are typically two outcomes:
-   They match your new salary, hooray!
-   They counteroffer with a lower amount or "just can't match." If their counteroffer is still higher than your true minimum, it's okay to accept, but you need to appear to think it over, ask for some time, and appear concerned or a bit deflated about it. You can typically squeeze an extra 1% out of them by saying things like, "They can't go ANY higher? Not even $1,000?"

Waiting
Don't worry about how long it takes them to get back to you—they haven't forgotten about you. If it's taking longer than expected, it's only because of internal red tape. This isn't some masterful freezing

tactic where they want to get you to come down and accept their original offer or anything like that.

That said, this is another reason why you need to position yourself to have several leads ready. If you're in the middle of negotiations with two acceptable potential jobs, then it won't matter if one is slow to respond or comes in lower than you'd be happy with.

The Employer Match

Some people advocate going back to your employer and trying to get them to match your new job offer. Why not, right? What's the worst that could happen? This is very dangerous. For one, it tips off your current employer to the fact that you've been looking and are therefore inherently disgruntled or disloyal. Secondly, your manager may simply not have the ability to match, and it will be an exercise in them showing you their lack of ability. The largest issue however is most employers don't believe money solves day-to-day work problems (or simply believe that you should be happy working where you are regardless of money). As a result they will always be suspicious of whether or not you're actually going to stay or take the money and run. I personally have seen at least one large payout result in the employee having no increased loyalty and leaving thirty days later.

I would only accept an offer that my current employer matched if I was okay with them thinking I was on borrowed time. Once they know you have no qualms about looking for a new job, they won't rely heavily on you for much longer—especially in leadership or high-level positions.

Extras!

Of course, there's more than salary that plays into the mix of an actual job offer. Don't ask for any of these up front, as you never want to let them know what's entirely on the table until the very end. Otherwise they'll play with all the dials at once instead of bumping salary to the max and then moving on to vacation days or a sign-on bonus. Talk salary, and ask to see the HR benefits. After salary is locked down, bring up vacation days and so forth.

Vacation days

Believe it or not, vacation days are some of the easiest things for most tech companies to give out. Some tech places won't even have official time off plans, and even if you do or don't negotiate extra time, it can all be moot if you have a flexible or rigid boss. The recruiters will try to act like these are a big deal. Don't believe them.

Any company with a start-up vibe is typical flexible with vacation times and sick days; any large company will usually have an established tracking system. In either scenario, the best predictor of your vacation time and sick day flexibility will be your direct boss. Standard paid leave is usually ten vacation days and three sick or personal days in your first year. Companies with well-established policies will also have some sort of accrual and bonus vacation time setup as you are there year over year (for example, three years means fifteen days' vacation time, etc.).

Vacation time is the soft drink of corporations—they cost very little to give out, but the corporation will act like they're expensive and worth a lot. If your recruiter begins padding vacation time in your offer, you can almost guarantee that they have a lax policy where vacation time doesn't matter or the bosses are very flexible.

Extra Remote Working Time

This is even worse than vacation days; unless it's a very large corporation, it's likely that the work-remote policy is very lax. The recruiters might act like you're special and could work remotely one day a week no problem, but maybe that's a standard at the office and you would have had it anyway. Even worse, you could negotiate a work-remote piece into your offer and then find out your coworkers and managers just don't believe that you're working.

Education Reimbursement

If any company offers you education reimbursement, typically it plays out like this: go to school on nights and weekends while you work for ACME, get a degree that's in ACME's field, and then you have to stay at ACME for three to four years after completing the degree or else you have to pay them back. In my opinion, this only makes education reimbursement worth it if you absolutely without a doubt HAVE to have the degree to proceed in your career, or you're absolutely certain you've found a fantastic job and can definitely work for them for three to four years.

Relocation

Most companies won't even offer relocation. If they do offer it, there are two types of relocation. Some companies will simply cut you a check for $5,000 or so and say, "See you in a few weeks." Great companies will handle the entire process for you, including paying for movers, putting you in temporary housing, and helping you sell your previous place and buy your new house/apartment. There's not much negotiating you can do here unfortunately— typically whatever package deal a company has is all they can offer you. Feel free to try to get a larger sign-on bonus if the relocation package stinks, though.

401(k) Match

In my experience, the different flavors of 401(k) matching aren't that different from each other, as this is a pretty basic perk. Sure, some companies have a very weak match, but more often than not the question is whether the company matches at all. If they do, it's usually at an acceptable level (somewhere around 3%). The difference in rate that company A or company B will match your 401(k) contribution is usually minimal.

Stock

Stock options, restricted stock, and stock in general usually takes around four years to vest fully. Each year you'll get 25% of your original allotment. Note that stock really isn't a solid offer until you find the job you want to settle down at. In your first ten to fifteen years in the job force, it's much more lucrative to have several jobs that last one to three years each. If you're playing along at home, that's below the four-year-minimum threshold for vesting. This makes stock less of a perk early in your career. Keep that in mind. Once you've reached a later stage in your career, stock and stock options actually become a viable incentive.

Health Benefits

The smaller the company, the more important it is to scrutinize their health benefits. Most large companies have a fairly popular healthcare provider whose benefits won't vary that much compared to their competition. Smaller companies and start-ups especially generally try to hire a younger workforce. Younger workforces use healthcare much less than older employees who typically have families. As a result, if you care about healthcare providers, it's particularly important to read through a smaller company's plan and consider it during negotiations. Note that you won't be able to change a company's benefits package regardless of company size. Your only move is to try to get a higher salary or sign-on if you don't like it.

Sign-on Bonus
These are surprisingly easy to get, but again you have to wait until after salary is locked down. Never mention what you think a normal sign-on bonus would be, just be vague and say, "Any kind of sign-on bonus would actually make me feel much better about the risk of changing jobs."

Never Forget They Want You!
They're talking to you because they are desperate; if they weren't desperate, they simply wouldn't even have communication open. The company may be slow in getting back to you or appear to be aloof, but that's the incompetence of their hiring process and/or gross bureaucracies of approval that must happen to hire anyone and not a sign that you've done anything wrong or that they've lost interest or are rescinding the offer.

Follow Up!
Make sure you leave things on very good terms with everyone involved, regardless of whether or not you accept the offer. That means basic social skills like smiling and waving goodbye to each person as you leave the office building. It means laughing at their dumb jokes. At this point, you should've added each person to your LinkedIn network at a minimum. You'll have no way of predicting who will move on from which job and remember you, or perhaps do a search and vaguely recognize your name. Throughout the negotiations, continue to be polite in all emails. There is literally no downside to leaving things on good terms with the recruiter, interviewers, and screeners when they decide to move on with someone else or if you politely decline their offer.

Chapter Nine:
Standards and Red Flags

Acceptance of prevailing standards often means we have no standards of our own. — Jean Toomer

Standards

So you've gotten your name out there. You managed to get a phone screen. You even got the interview and managed to negotiate a great job offer and sign-on bonus. But a job isn't just an offer letter. Up to this point, *Novice Negotiator* has focused on what you can do to capture what appears to be the best possible job on paper. Most of the focus has been on what you as a candidate can do to highlight your strengths and how to strike the best bargain.

What I haven't addressed is that even though Company X may have the best salary, there can be enormous problems in working there. Beyond a paycheck, the day to day might just be too awful to bear.

In this chapter I'll go over all the pitfalls that you might see during the phone screen and interview process so as to avoid that disastrous job. Some of alarming details can be hard to pick up on if you haven't had personal experience with them in the past. If you have the luxury of passing over an offer because of one of the pitfalls below, that's great. If you don't have that luxury, at least you'll have a better understanding of what you might be getting into.

I'll be reviewing various job standards that would normally take a person years of working experience to figure out.

Reviews, Career Pathing

Almost no start-up or small company will have any career pathing of any kind. Several will adopt a third-party cookie-cutter review system where you get rated on five generic skills on a scale from 1 to 5, with the average rating being 3.5 for nearly every single employee no matter what.

Larger companies try to have something a bit more formal, but typically this just means you have two to three "goals" that you have to complete by the end of each year. It's quite rare that free trainings or certifications are given and even rarer that a company will send its employees to conferences. When you factor in travel costs like hotels and airfare, conferences get incredibly pricey, so much so that it's just not likely that you'll be the ONE person they send. Thankfully, none of the advice in this book revolves around playing the "certification game" where you get certified for everything under the sun and hope something gets picked up by a bot searching résumés. On the other hand, this means that regardless of what career pathing and review system, or lack thereof, is in place, your job growth and mentorship will be 100% related to the personality and effort of your boss. This is another reason it's good to ask, "How big is the team?" during the interview process. If the person in charge of you also has to manage fourteen other people, it's highly unlikely that you will get any attention with regards to job growth.

Annual Bonuses
It may seem strange to bring up annual bonuses during an interview for a job you don't even have yet, and personally I do not recommend bringing it up yourself. It's more likely that the recruiter will dangle a potential 10% raise year over year or some other completely unguaranteed number.

For yearly bonuses, 3–5% is the new standard. If you're not getting that amount at your current job, begin to look immediately. It will take you years to make the same amount you make in your current role versus just changing jobs within the next few months and having a larger salary immediately. Always compare your bonus to what you can get at a new job instead. Until very late in your career, moving jobs should always be more lucrative than staying and getting a raise. Typically a sign-on bonus plus a natural increase in salary at a new job will be much, much more than your current company will be willing to offer.

This same rule applies to internal promotions. Generally your boss will use the word "promotion" in four scenarios: (1) When they just want you to do more work and can't actually afford to pay you anymore—a promotion "in name only"; (2) when your annual bonus is greater than their generic amount and they had to justify it on paper to the bosses above them; (3) when you're a stellar employee and they're worried you're going to leave; and (4) when they actually are rewarding you for doing a great job by expanding your role and compensation (this does happen sometimes, I swear!).

As you can see, this is why it's so important to counter any offer letter. If you can get a 2–3% raise out of the gate, then you're essentially a full year ahead on your career path with regards to salary. It's incredibly easy to get a 2–3% bump in your offer letter. It's actually quite difficult to fight for a raise once you're already inside and working for Company X.

As mentioned before, unless you're part of a massive company with thousands of employees, there likely isn't some salary equation. This is particularly relevant here. If you signed on at $70,000 but all of your peers are making $100,000, there will be no "correction" or "adjustment" by your boss. Year after year they'll just give you 3%. It's just how budgets work. Your boss's boss will look and say "30% increase? That's insane, no way."

Budget Buckets and Salaries

To go further behind the curtain, I'm going to dive into department budgets briefly. Once you understand this, you'll realize your manager's promises are capped and outside of his or her control. The first item to note is that obviously, budgets are earmarked for various purposes. This can be just good accounting, tax regulations, or simply how the finances of a certain company are managed, but generally speaking, budgets for various areas are separated into buckets.

Why does this matter? Let's just look at department budgets as an example. There are monthly or quarterly or annual allowances that individual departments are given for things like tickets for tech conferences, taking the team out for lunch, or handling various travel expenses. Another bucket under a department is how much they're allotted annually for raises. Think about that for a second. Your entire department has been allotted a fixed dollar amount for raises. This now means that even though your performance isn't directly tied to Susan or John who aren't even on your team, your raises are linked. The more John gets, the less there is for Susan, and the less there is for you.

Regardless of how well you do, there is a fixed cap on what your boss can give you. You probably knew that, at least in the back of your mind. Additionally, your other team members will indirectly limit how much of a raise you can get. This ugly thought isn't brought up much, as no manager in their right mind wants to sow discord among a team. As a result, there's a weird and delicate balancing act where the solidly performing team members are given the minimum that their boss thinks will keep them around for another year, while the all-stars are given a tad more. There's just rarely enough to go around.

If everyone on the team did an outstanding job in a given year, there's still only a fixed amount of dollars to dish out.

The moral of the story is to take whatever you can with raises and bonuses while you're at a certain job, but never count on them. It's always easier to increase your salary with a job change.

Red Flags
Below I've put together a few phrases you may hear during the interview that sound fine or even great on the surface. But from past experience, I can safely say that these can actually be warning signs. Note that I would never automatically shut down a job offer if I saw any of these red flags, but during the negotiation process, I would weigh them against other possible offers. Factor the warnings in as you negotiate. You'll have to determine for yourself personally how much money you're willing to accept in order to deal with the possible shortcomings of a job (and for how long you're willing to stick it out). Also, I have not included any obvious red flags like the interviewer telling you the job is terrible. We're only focusing on the ones that sound good on the surface but may actually be dangerous to those who haven't encountered them before.

"We have no vacation policy, take as much as you want."
Those who haven't heard this before may think it sounds great. Typically, unlimited vacation actually means they have no HR system at all for tracking vacation time. Still sound good? Well, the way it plays out in reality is that you're never allowed to take vacation time because there's always a project going out the door. Without a system of recording time, you can't schedule time off in

advance appropriately, and everyone is guilt-tripped into working every day possible.

It also means if your boss FEELS like you're taking too much vacation, then you are—even if you're taking less vacation than everyone else. While this policy will work for people very close to the top of an organization, it's actually quite detrimental for most employees, especially at small start-ups where it's easy to notice when someone isn't in the office.

"We have catered lunches every day."
Sounds great for someone right out of college, doesn't it? Don't think for a moment that there isn't a business risk analysis done before a company decides to offer lunch every day. This strategic plan usually is used to keep people working through lunch. If you don't go out to eat, then you're available in-office to handle any fires immediately. Be warned that you'll likely be working long hours at any job that offers daily or near-daily free lunch. The worst part is that you eventually get tired of the catering companies regardless and after a while won't even use the free food part of the perk.

"We're a flat organization."
This is code for "There is no career path for you here." So-called "flat" organizations just mean that companies are double-dipping and expect you to perform management-level duties as well as your actual day-to-day project deliverables. In these companies, there is typically a very high level of management and then several individual contributors immediately below them. Want a raise or a good review? Need flexibility with time off? Have an HR problem with a coworker? You better be on the good side of founders, because they're likely the only ones who can do anything at all to

help you. Also, you likely will be seen as "causing trouble" or "not a team player" if you go against the grain of a "flat" organization.

Knowing it for what it is, though, you can still get lots of experience at a place that thinks middle managers are pointless. Usually you'll have lots of responsibility and autonomy, they just won't reward you for it unless you impress a specific individual (instead of hitting your goals or having a career plan). The best plan of attack here is to learn new technologies and create custom solutions while you're at said job, and then leverage that on your résumé to get a higher-level role in your next job elsewhere. It will be quite rare that you'd get promoted from within at a flat company.

Chapter Ten:
The New Job and How to Keep Going

Even though I've had the body of work I've had, and the success I've had, I do not rest on my laurels whatsoever. —Jonathan Rhys Meyers

In this chapter, I'll be discussing how to continue networking and what the passive job-hunting cycle looks like after you've started your new job. In tech, the average tenure is a little over a year—shocking I know. This all but dispels the job-hopper myth. If you're good, they'll come find you. You need to be ready.

Continue Networking

During the first few weeks of onboarding at a new job, you'll get dragged to numerous meetings. Even if they're boring, you can still use them to your advantage. Be an outgoing member of society and politely introduce yourself to new faces. After the meetings, take the invite list and search for the names on LinkedIn. Add everyone. It's good to do this regularly. As a rule, anyone I have a business meeting with, I later add to my LinkedIn network. Meet a few folks in another far away department? Add them. Have a call with a vendor you just met? Add them. Don't be shy. Some won't add you back. Some will. It's good to keep your network growing.

Update Your Résumé: Monthly Journal

Keep a monthly tab on all the projects you're working on. This will be great for performance reviews at the end of the year, but it will be best for when you have to update your résumé and need to list out all the initiatives you worked on. Keep track of things like if you hired anyone, what technologies and other teams you worked with, a few one-liners describing the actual projects, and any other things you may have worked on. We've all been through that "ugh" feeling of trying to remember things when updating our résumé. Be prepared by doing it regularly

Referrals and References

Did your current interviewers ask for references? Unfortunately, you can't just keep using the same one or two people from a job you had years ago. Recruiters always want the latest possible references you have available. Keep that in mind throughout your months and years at this new job. Who would recommend you to a future employer? Who would possibly reach out to you with a job referral if they left for a great new company? You don't have to be friends with everybody, but it helps to have at least a few close strong players in your pocket.

Going "Off the Market" and "The Quick Hop"
Some people I know refuse to even entertain the thought of responding to new recruiters the moment they start a new job. This can be a mistake. Most head hunters will actually reach out to people who have just changed jobs. It's one of the easiest times to get a candidate. Why? Because you have zero baked-in loyalty to your new employer. You just got there. Unless you know you scored your dream job, stay active on the market for at least a month. You can get a quick-hop and yet another bump in salary and benefits almost immediately. Of course, follow the same tips and tricks laid out in earlier chapters that got you to this point in the first place. This time you'll have much greater leverage since everyone knows you could just stay at this new job you just landed.

Year-Over-Year Plan: When to Actively Look

First Year
Aim to get a promotion, with salary increase if possible, otherwise, in name only—you'll want a title change of some sort for your résumé. Get involved in new projects. Start projects yourself (on your own time at first, then later maybe they'll let you do it on company time). At large corporations, they likely have policies on how long you have to be there before you get a promotion, and a raise is probably within a very small range for first-year employees.

Second Year

Begin to look for two things during your second year: leadership roles at your current job, and a new job at other companies. At a minimum, you'll want your résumé to show that your responsibilities increased. Continue to start new initiatives, and focus on items that improve productivity or performance. Any type of process enhancement looks great on a résumé. With regards to a new job, get used to talking to recruiters again and positioning yourself favorably. I only recommend starting to look for new jobs. I don't recommend making a move in the middle of your second year unless you think you've locked down a large salary bump or found a dream job. Definitely don't settle for a lateral move at this stage.

At the end of the second year, compare your performance review, raise, and/or promotion to your first year. Hopefully you can get a solid bump in either your first or second year, regardless of company culture.

Third Year

If you still love your job, great! I would start to evaluate your long-term potential there. Consider whether or not you could stomach a re-org if they haven't had one yet. I would expect there to be a shift in upper-level management at least once every four years. If you like your job mainly because you like your boss, or you like one or two other people, be cautious. One company re-org can really upset the status quo. On the other hand, if you like the majority people at your job, you can probably withstand a re-org or two.

If you plan on staying through to your fourth year at a tech job, it's important to know that you're implicitly making a decision to stay and start to become an "old timer." This is perfectly acceptable if you're later in your career. In the first ten to fifteen years, however, it's much more lucrative to stay one to three years at different tech jobs as you build your network and diversify your skillset and experiences. Once you hit the fifteen to twenty-five year mark, it's prudent to decide if there's a job where you can have a more permanent role, as ageism will begin to heavily deter your possible options unless you're seen as an absolute expert in a cutting-edge technology.

More Career Advice

The following are some tricks and tips to help you during your actual day-to-day at your new job. From a career perspective, there are some generic things you can do regardless of your role that will put you in a good light. You may naturally already achieve these or perhaps you avoid doing them because you really value your home life. That's okay, these things aren't for everybody. But it should be at least helpful to educate yourself on how much perception plays into your regular evaluations from management.

Extra Fifteen Minutes

When you can afford to, work slightly longer hours. If you stay an extra fifteen minutes each day, it can appear that you're working really hard. Just like the interview process, there aren't a lot of hard criteria for your boss's boss to judge you during reviews. However if you're seen as one of the people that stay late regularly, it can be an easy way to get a raise. The reverse of this is true. Believe it or not, leaving a few minutes before 5 p.m. each day can really impact their perception of you if they're old-fashioned enough. You may be progressive, but your bosses and their bosses are likely to be much older and have more traditional ideas.

After-Hours Emails

Related to the staying slightly late at work, send an after-hours email once every other month or so (unless the opportunity comes up naturally otherwise). If there's an email thread you can reply to from home after 7 p.m. every once in a while, it help paints the picture that you're a workaholic. Whether you actually want to be a workaholic or not is up to you, but the appearance alone is worth a lot.

The Danger of Working Remotely

Remember that when it comes to promotions, your manager will have to get approval from their manager. It will be one gut feeling that's validated by a second gut feeling at a higher pay grade. Unfortunately, what this means is if you're not in the office a lot, your boss's boss won't see you in the hallway, won't see you in random meetings, won't see you around talking to other people and doing things that appear to look like work. While you won't get a promotion if you don't have the skillset, your perceived work ethic weighs in heavily here too. This is another reason that working remotely isn't necessarily a perk. I wouldn't recommend working from home more than once a month if you're trying to fast-track your career. If you're just trying to punch the clock and get paid, however, go nuts and work from home.

Tackling Work Projects

Let's follow this theme of soft skills and attitude carrying way more weight than people realize and apply it to how you tackle your work projects. If there's a large initiative that is cross departmental or that simply involves lots of people, if you're able to be the person who "helps everybody no matter what," that will go really far with management-level individuals. It's just a great policy in general during your career. Not everyone has the personality for it, and you may flat-out not want to be the one who is stuck doing other people's actual work, but if you're trying to make a great impression and can handle the extra effort it takes to have this attitude, it can really pay off come promotion/raise/annual review time.

Outside of Work: Meetups, Conferences, and Passion Projects
While the main way of building a reputation in the tech work is simply via references from a past job, there are alternate channels and communities you can become involved in that will lead to lucrative job offers as well. Ask your boss if you can host a local Meetup at work—something on topic in the world of tech that you can speak to and invite others to. Getting your name out there and networking in this fashion is incredibly valuable. At these events, exchange emails, LinkedIn profiles, and any other professional social media accounts you're comfortable sharing.

Besides Meetups, apply to speak at a conference. This may sound daunting. If you're not a public speaker or are simply terrified of talking in front of large crowds, feel free to skip this one. But actually becoming a speaker at a conference is easier than it sounds. While some conferences do in fact seek out individuals, most have an application process where you simply submit your talk. If it's well written, you may just be in. Clearly this way of getting your name out there is fantastic for your tech reputation. Your job will likely love that you're speaking, since it will give them more credibility at said conference.

Finally, try to have a passion project—something you spend time coding after work hours; something tech-related that you can share publicly. It's a great interview talking point, and if anyone else uses your little pet project, then you've just increased your street cred.

*   *   *   *   *

There you have it—you're now a novice negotiator! Knowing and using the information in this book puts you far ahead of most of your peers. If there's one nugget of advice I could give to sum up this whole book, it's not to underestimate the importance of practice. If you do nothing else, simply go on a lot of interviews for the practice. Interviewing (and negotiating) is a learned skill, just like anything else. The nerves, the confusion, being stumped on answers, being confident asking for what you want—it all goes away the more you practice.

Remember, the tech industry job market wavers up and down but it's never truly that bad, and there's always something available. Get out there, and get negotiating! Good luck!